# DESIGNING GROUPWORK

# DESIGNING GROUPWORK

## Strategies for the Heterogeneous Classroom

ELIZABETH G. COHEN

Foreword by John I. Goodlad

Teachers College, Columbia University
New York and London

Published by Teachers College Press, 1234 Amsterdam Avenue, New York, N.Y. 10027

*Library of Congress Cataloging-in-Publication Data*

Cohen, Elizabeth G., 1931–
  Designing groupwork.

  Bibliography: p.
  Includes index.
  1. Group work in education.  2.  Interaction analysis in education.  I.  Title.
LB1032.C56  1986      371.3'95      86-14502


ISBN 0-8077-2816-0

*Manufactured in the United States of America*

96  95  94  93  92  91          9  8  7  6  5

To the Stanford School of Education graduate students
who taught me about schools

# Contents

# Foreword

Goals for schools—whether at local, state, or national levels—suggest to the reader an active learning process in classrooms. One conjures up visions of students exchanging viewpoints on issues, checking the validity of diverse views through reading, sharing their findings, and preparing individual and group reports. Research shows that teachers generally perceive as desirable such practices as student involvement in setting goals, student interaction in small groups, and student involvement in ongoing classroom dialogue.

Alas, research reveals teaching practices and learning opportunities that fall far short of these expectations and ideals. Teachers lecture, explain to, and question the total class and monitor seatwork most of the time, especially in secondary schools. It has been found, for example, that teachers far out-talk *all* of their students together during 150 minutes of daily talk recorded in hundreds of classrooms. During these 150 minutes, students initiated talk through unsolicited comments or questions very rarely, such initiations consuming some seven or eight minutes on the whole.

Teachers rarely question the validity of such findings. Usually, they recognize themselves in the data and become uncomfortable; some become defensive. But most teachers quickly move beyond defensiveness into questions of how to proceed differently. They know there are other ways. Indeed, many have engaged in an internal struggle brought about by the shortfall between their own perceptions of what good teaching is and daily circumstances that seem to frustrate methods other than those they most often observed when they were students. And some wince over the memories of brief forays into alternatives: total class discussions dominated by a few aggressive students, small group sessions that got out of hand, and so-called cooperative learning endeavors that exacerbated incipient racism. They have no desire to repeat those disasters.

For a long time, I have been looking for something useful to put into the heads and hands of teachers who recognize the need to go beyond the conventional ways of teaching described above—and especially those whose brief experiments with alternatives have been less than satisfying. Principles alone will not suffice. Prescriptions, devoid of understanding, undoubtedly will lead to more disasters.

Elizabeth Cohen's book, *Designing Groupwork: Strategies for the Heterogeneous Classroom*, comes closer to what I have been seeking than any sources known to me. First, it is an almost ideal blend of theory and practice, with principle bridging the two and specific examples clarifying the applicability of these principles. Second, in addition to providing ample research support for the general concepts of groupwork introduced early on, specific research studies are then used to document the usefulness of practices derived from these concepts. Third, the illustrations range widely over ages and grades, subjects, special problems likely to be encountered, and processes to be used. Fourth, there is surprising sensitivity to the step-by-step training needs of teachers venturing into using groupwork as a way to maximize students' learning. My surprise stems not from Cohen's background (her research interests often have been guided by precisely this sensitivity) but from firsthand experiences with the difficulty of being this practical while remaining true to basic principles. One is reminded once again of the practicality of good theory.

Overall, what Elizabeth Cohen succeeds in doing is to provide a technology—in the very best sense of rigorously linking a practical human endeavor with knowledge bearing on that endeavor—in a pedagogical domain that has tended to defy such rigor. Although Cohen illustrates many different uses for this technology, she makes clear at the outset that groupwork is only one way to provide students with meaningful encounters with knowledge. She views groupwork as particularly relevant to the higher order cognitive processes and to goals stressing democratic values. One is brought back to the writings of John Dewey and the enormous impact of his works on the thinking of educators. But efforts to translate this thinking into a technology have suffered either in not going beyond principles or in rigidity and prescription. As I stated earlier, Cohen manages to provide a technology without falling victim to either of these two shortcomings—a rare and valuable contribution, indeed.

There is no point in my summarizing what the author has to say about each of the many themes and topics in her book. This is best left for the reader to peruse and reflect upon. For the reader interested in knowing why group approaches to student learning are useful, what is encompassed by the term "groupwork," and how to proceed with a class, not much is missing. The book has something for a wide range of readers, but clearly it is intended for and will be most useful to teachers.

One theme of schooling is emerging with such critical importance, however, that I am impelled to say something about Cohen's treatment of it. Even though most schools are structured for purposes of reducing the heterogeneity of the student populations with which teachers must deal—through tracking and the separation of "special" students into segregated groups—the problems experienced by teachers in dealing with individual differences appear to be increasing. Part of the difficulty arises out of the fact that organizational arrangements seeking group homogeneity are crude mechanisms that create more problems than they solve. The inequities produced are such that corrective actions soon will be taken through the courts if schools and communities fail to redress them. The difficulties also grow out of the changing pupil populations in which it appears that increasing numbers of students are at the margins and at risk. We are running out of organizational and special grouping types of solutions.

Cohen effectively argues the case for groupwork in heterogeneous classes and provides useful examples of how students are drawn naturally into learning from one another, regardless of their differing levels of attainment. Indeed, these differences become assets rather than liabilities. The principles underlying groupwork presented in the early chapters come into play most effectively as she points clear directions through issues complicated by special interests and often charged with emotion and bias. Teachers who have become increasingly uncomfortable with tracking, for example, will be both encouraged and helped in learning to proceed with an appealing, defensible alternative.

Prior to receiving the manuscript of *Designing Groupwork*, I had resolved to write no more forewords or introductions to books (except for those of former students). But I knew that Elizabeth Cohen's book would reflect a lifetime of serious study and reflection on schools and classrooms, and so I accepted her invitation (albeit rather reluctantly) to read the manuscript and write the Foreword. It was a good decision because the time spent was negligible when compared with what I learned.

John I. Goodlad
May, 1986

# Acknowledgments

The early work on this book was supported by the National Institute of Education, Grant no. OB-NIE-G-78-0212 (P-4).

The artist is Anne Finkelstein.

I am grateful for the careful reading and constructive criticism of Annike Bredo, Susan Rosenholtz, Theresa Perez, Rachel Lotan, and my sister and favorite editor, Miriam Finkelstein.

I would also like to acknowledge the assistance and influence of Cecilia Navarrete, who brought to me so much understanding of the exigencies of classroom life as well as insights concerning the education of the language minority student. Her work on classroom ecology provided many of the suggestions I offer in my discussion of that subject in Chapter 5.

Finally, I am grateful to the many classroom teachers who have worked with me in using these techniques, helping a sociologist develop useful knowledge for the practitioner.

# DESIGNING GROUPWORK

# 1 Groupwork as a Strategy for Classrooms

"Why didn't they tell me when I was in teacher training that children learn by talking and working together?" asked a third-grade teacher who has tried groups at learning centers for the first time. Have you ever noticed that you learn more about concepts and ideas when you talk, explain, and argue about them with others than when you listen to a lecture or read a book? Although many adults realize that this is so, very few classrooms allow students to talk together. This is a book for teachers who want to know how to make this principle of adult learning work for students of all ages. If a teacher wants to produce active learning, then groupwork, properly designed, is a powerful tool for providing simultaneous opportunities for all class members.

Small groups are not a panacea for all instructional problems. They are only one tool, useful for specific kinds of teaching goals and especially relevant for classrooms with a wide mix of student academic and linguistic skills. The choice of groupwork as a strategy depends upon what the teacher is trying to achieve. Most teachers will want to use groups in combination with a variety of other classroom formats for different tasks.

## WHAT IS GROUPWORK?

This book defines groupwork as students working together in a group small enough so that everyone can participate on a task that has been clearly assigned. Moreover, students are expected to carry out their task without direct and immediate supervision of the teacher. Groupwork is not the same as ability grouping in which the teachers divide up the class by academic criteria so that they can instruct a more homogeneous group. It should also be distinguished from small groups that teachers compose for intensive instruction, such as the flexible grouping procedures often used in individualized reading instruction.

When teachers give students a group task and allow them to make mistakes and struggle on their own, they have delegated authority. This is a key feature of groupwork. Delegating authority in an instructional task makes students responsible for specific parts of their work; students are free to accomplish their task in the way they think best, but they are accountable to the teacher for the final product. Delegating authority does not mean that the learning process is uncontrolled; the teacher maintains control through evaluation of the final product.

In contrast to delegation of authority is the more common practice of direct supervision. The teacher exercising direct supervision tells students what their task is and how to do it. She monitors the students closely to prevent them from making mistakes and to correct any errors right away.

The question of who is in charge of the group is critical; if a teacher is in charge, regardless of the age and maturity of the students, the teacher will do more talking than the students. The teacher's evaluation of each member's performance will have far more weight than that of any other group member. If the teacher plays the role of a direct supervisor of group activity, members will talk, not to each other, but to the teacher as the authority figure who is overseeing performance. Group members will want to know what the teacher expects them to say and will be mostly interested in finding out what the teacher thinks of their performance. Even if the teacher assigns a task to the group but hovers nearby waiting to intervene at the first misstep or sign of confusion, she is not delegating authority; she is using direct supervision.

A second key feature of groupwork is that members need

each other to some degree to complete the task; they cannot do it all by themselves. Students take over some of the teaching function by suggesting what other people should do, by listening to what other people are saying, and by deciding how to get the job done within the time and resource limitations set by the instructor.

Students in a group communicate about their task with each other. This may include asking questions, explaining, making suggestions, criticizing, listening, agreeing, disagreeing, or making joint decisions. Interaction may also be nonverbal, such as pointing, showing how, nodding, frowning, or smiling.

The process of group interaction is enormously interesting to students. Students who usually do anything but what they are asked to do become actively involved with their work and are held there by the action of the group. There are several reasons why this is so. Face-to-face interaction with other group members demands a response or, at least, attentive behavior. In addition, students care very much about evaluations of classmates; they do not want to let the group down by refusing to participate. Lastly, peers provide assistance so a student does not become hopelessly confused about what he or she is supposed to do. Students who are disengaged from their work in the classroom are often students who do not understand their assignments.

Although groupwork has potential for learning, talking and working together with peers is the source of a whole series of problems. Neither children nor adults necessarily know how to work successfully in the group setting. American culture, in particular, provides very few opportunities to learn group skills. These problems can be overcome with proper preparation of the task and of the students. This volume presents both problems and suggested solutions.

## THE TEACHER AS EDUCATIONAL ENGINEER

Contrary to what most practitioners believe, there is nothing so practical as a good theory. Sociologists and social psychologists have useful theories and relevant research on small groups in laboratory and classroom settings. From these theories and research have come some general principles applicable to the instructor's situation. Using these principles, you can analyze your class and your goals in order to design a suitable small group format. These same general principles suggest ways to evaluate the success of the technique so that you can decide whether it works for your class, and in what way it can be improved for next time.

The advantage of general principles is that they can be used in any classroom from elementary to college level. The particulars can be simply adapted or engineered for differences in age of the students and in the nature of the setting. The general principles continue to guide the design. For example, the simplicity of the instructions will vary with the age of the students, as will the analysis of what skills group members already have in comparison to what they will need for the group task. It is clear that in younger groups there are potential problems of discipline and classroom management that are absent for older groups. Such differences may mean that the teacher will need to spend a longer time preparing students and that the groups will move much more slowly in completing their task, but principles such as delegation of authority and having the students teach each other remain the same.

## USE OF RESEARCH

Most relevant for this book is the research that has applied useful theories to classrooms. In some cases, the theory and the research are sufficiently strong to say with some confidence that there are specific desirable effects of groupwork on student behavior. As a professor of education who is also a research sociologist, I have directed classroom research for many years. This research has centered on team teaching, treatment of interracial status problems in the classroom, and managing groupwork in academically and linguistically heterogeneous classrooms. Many of the techniques for groupwork come from these research situations, where they have proven to be highly effective. The two elementary school settings where most of this groupwork research took place were desegregated classrooms and bilingual classrooms.

During my years of classroom research, I have always worked closely with teachers who have left the classroom for graduate work. Many of the dissertations of these teachers are the best sources of evidence in the book. It has always been these graduate students who tried to make research relevant and practical for the classroom instructor; they have coaxed me from the laboratory to the infinitely more complex and challenging world of the classroom.

As a teacher of beginning secondary school teachers, I have used some of the materials in this book to help my students design groupwork for their classrooms. Some of the examples in the text are taken from their projects.

## HOW TRUE ARE THE PRINCIPLES?

Experienced practitioners obviously want to know how true my assertions are for their own classrooms. Will these ideas work in all settings? What are the dangers of things going wrong? Are the risks worth the gains and the extra work?

Let me be perfectly frank: I do not know for sure whether the principles hold under all conditions. But I do know of a variety of classroom conditions where the data support the propositions I have set out. What the practitioner must do is think about what is likely to happen when these principles are applied. There is no way that a set of recipes in a book will relieve the instructor of this responsibility. If it appears that nothing untoward is likely to happen, then it may well be worth the risk and the extra effort to try and accomplish certain teaching goals that cannot be reached in any other way.

# 2 Why Groupwork?

Groupwork is an effective technique for achieving certain kinds of intellectual and social learning goals. It is a superior technique for conceptual learning, for creative problem solving, and for increasing oral language proficiency. Socially, it will improve intergroup relations by increasing trust and friendliness. It will teach students skills for working in groups that can be transferred to many student and adult work situations. Groupwork is also a strategy for solving two common classroom problems: keeping students involved with their work, and managing students with a wide range of academic skills.

## INTELLECTUAL GOALS

Groupwork can help students learn academically, as in this example of Geraldo learning about magnification.

Geraldo watches the other children as they complete their task of making a water drop lens. "What do you see?" Geraldo asks another child, as he tries to peer into the finished lens. The other child looks up and lets Geraldo look more carefully at it. Geraldo very eagerly goes back to his own lens-making task. He appears to be having trouble taping a piece of clear plastic on a white index card with a hole in the middle; he keeps getting the plastic bunched up on the tape instead of getting the tape to hold the plastic on top of the card. "Oh, shoot!" Geraldo says and gets up to see what another child is doing in constructing her lens. He returns to his task only to be distracted by the child next to him. "Oooh, it gets bigger!" she exclaims. Geraldo gets up and looks at her water drop lens. He raises his eyebrows and very quickly goes back and finishes his lens. Geraldo appears to have understood what the problem was in completing the lens because he rapidly tapes it together

6

without any further trouble. He now reaches over and takes the eye dropper from a glass filled with water. He very carefully fills it with water, centers it over his lens card and squirts one drop over the plastic where the hole is cut. Apparently satisfied with what he did he puts the excess water in the eye dropper back in the jar. He gets a piece of cloth to examine under his lens. The water slides around the plastic covering the paper and he cries out, "Oh, no!" He puts his lens down, straightens out the cloth and then carefully slides the lens on top of the cloth. He very slowly looks into his lens and shouts out, "Oooh—bad—oooh!" "What did you see?" asks one of the girls. "Look how big mine got," says Geraldo. "What are you going to write?" she asks. Geraldo looks into the lens again and says, "It gets bigger." He then takes other flat objects and places his water drop lens on top of each one. As he looks at each object with his lens, he nods his head and says, "Yep!" Talking to himself he says, "They all get bigger." He looks at the girl he has been talking with and finally asks her, "Did yours get bigger too?" (Navarrete, 1980, pp. 13–14)

Geraldo has discovered the principle of magnification. The process has not been an easy one, and he would never have been successful without the assistance of a classmate working on the same task. Just being able to watch others at work gave him some important information. And being able to talk things over seemed to help even further. Notice that Geraldo understands the idea in such a way that he can apply it to a new setting—when he is able to understand a concept in a new setting, we know that he has a true grasp of the abstract idea.

How else could Geraldo have learned about magnification? Could he have understood it through a teacher's explanation? By reading about it? By completing some paper-and-pencil exercises on the subject? In order for him to understand much at all the materials and talk would have to be in English and Spanish, but Geraldo has limited reading skills in both languages. It is unlikely that he would grasp the idea in such a way that he could transfer it to new settings. In the setting where this interaction was recorded, Geraldo had access to instructions in English, Spanish, and pictographs; he also had access to Spanish-speaking as well as English-speaking classmates and to teachers who spoke both languages. A major advantage of combining a manipulative task with a group setting is that Geraldo has a number of helpful resources, including concrete materials to represent abstract ideas and other people engaged in the same task. He can watch them; he can ask them questions; he can discuss and argue with them; he can try to explain things; and he can demonstrate ideas nonverbally with the materials. Most importantly, Geraldo is allowed to struggle on his own, to make his own mistakes. No adult rushes in to tell him what to do and to give him a verbal explanation—such assistance might well have short-circuited his discovery.

## Conceptual Learning

After an instructor has introduced new concepts and has illustrated how they apply, students must obtain some active practice in using these new ideas and in applying them in various ways. This is as true for students in my graduate seminar as it was for Geraldo, a fourth grader. Traditional methods of accomplishing these goals include written papers, written exercises during class time (seatwork), and large group instruction. During question-and-answer activities teachers ask the students questions, and one student at a time tries to answer, while the rest of the class listens.

There are obvious limitations to these techniques. Clearly, when recitation is used, only one student at a time gets the active practice. There is no evidence that listening to other people assimilate new concepts is the same experience as doing it for oneself. Exercises and essays are the time-honored methods of teachers everywhere. Yet low achievers and less-motivated students are often reluctant to do these prescribed exercises and may complete them partially, if at all. If the teacher assigns the work during class, these students are very likely to be disengaged from their task (Berliner et al., 1978). If the teacher assigns homework, many students, especially in schools with a poor climate for learning and in classes in the lower-level tracks in high school, will fail to do it.

Even among the better-motivated high school students,

essay assignments or written reports have their limitations. Understanding and assimilating new concepts and writing about them demand both cognitive processes and writing skills. Problems with writing are compounded with problems of thinking. Take, for example, the high school biology student who writes: "In the case of chlorophyll, photosynthesis will take place." Does the student understand that photosynthesis cannot take place without chlorophyll? The teacher can only guess about the student's understanding of the process. Furthermore, until the student gets back the corrected essay or exercise, there is no chance to discover confusion and error. As every busy instructor knows, the lag between a student's turning in a paper and receiving it back with adequate comments may be embarrassingly long.

Groupwork can be more effective than these traditional methods for gaining a proper understanding of abstract concepts. This is not to say that groupwork under all conditions will be more effective. Two basic conditions must be met for groupwork to facilitate conceptual learning:

- The learning task should require conceptual thinking rather than learning to apply a rule or memorization.
- The group must have the resources to complete the assignment successfully. These include intellectual skills, vocabulary, relevant information, and properly prepared task instructions.

Many classroom tasks simply require the student to memorize material or rules. After memorizing the rule, they must learn to recognize a problem as a place to apply the rule. Examples of such routine tasks in the early elementary years are memorizing number facts or learning to apply a rule such as: drop the final "e" before adding "ing" to a word. In contrast are the tasks of reading comprehension or understanding the principles underlying computation; these call for more conceptual thinking. In secondary school there are also many tasks requiring memorization or rule application. Students memorize certain vocabulary and facts of science or learn to solve a set of math problems that all have the same format by using an

algorithm or rule. In contrast, hypothesizing about lab experiments or analyzing sentence structures are more conceptual
tasks.

There is no particular advantage in giving a group a set
of routine computational examples to complete. They will respond by doing the most sensible thing—copying the answers
of the student who is best and fastest at computation. The same
thing will happen if you give the group a quiz to complete on
facts of science or history. Contrast these examples with assigning a group the task of solving a difficult word problem in
arithmetic, discovering what makes a battery in a flashlight
work, interpreting a passage of literature, understanding the
phototropic behavior of plants, deciding what is wrong with the
grammatical construction of some sentences, role-playing historical events, or learning how to plot a set of coordinates.
These are all examples of conceptual tasks that can be highly
effective in the group setting.

In tasks that are conceptual, students will interact in a way
that assists them in understanding and applying ideas. Researchers have been able to show that group interaction has a
favorable effect on understanding mathematical concepts and
on reading comprehension. In bilingual classrooms where
children were talking about and working together on tasks using math and science concepts that demanded thinking skills,
the more they talked and worked together, the more they
learned how to do word problems (Cohen & Intili, 1981).

Exactly how does talking and working together assist conceptual learning? A number of research studies provide important clues to how this process works. Webb (1982)
emphasizes the benefits of explaining to others, especially when
the material is complex and requires integration or reorgani-
zation. Putting concepts into words in the context of explaining to a peer is particularly helpful for concept attainment
(Durling & Shick, 1976).

The student who does not initially understand the concept also stands to gain from the peer process. Children who
receive help improve their achievement test scores, depending
upon the quality of the help they receive (Webb, 1982). Even
kindergarten children have been shown to learn very abstract

concepts when placed in a group with peers who already understand the idea (Murray, 1972).

Disagreement and intellectual conflict are a desirable part of the interaction in a problem-solving group. Johnson and Johnson (1979), who have worked extensively with cooperative learning groups in classrooms, state that conceptual conflict resulting from controversy in the group forces individuals to consider new information and to gain cognitive understanding in a way that will transfer to new settings. Exposure to different points of view in an interaction helps children to examine their environment more objectively and to use other perspectives than their own; it helps them to reach a more advanced stage of cognitive development, as described by Piaget (Piaget, 1951, 1970; Inhelder, Sinclair, & Bovet, 1974; Sharan & Sharan, 1976).

In review, if a teacher's goal is conceptual learning, properly structured group tasks can be an important aid. However, the task must be correctly selected, and the students must have access to the necessary vocabulary and resources to achieve a required level of intellectual discourse. There is no point to a discussion that represents collective ignorance. Furthermore, there must be some way to be sure that people will listen carefully to each other, explain to each other, and provide some corrective feedback for each other. All this is unlikely to take place by magic; the teacher has to lay the groundwork through meticulous planning, as is discussed in Chapters 4 and 5.

## Creative Problem Solving

Ed and Carl (eight and seven years old, respectively) are trying to figure out how a balance scale works:

*Ed*: Now [let's start].
*Carl*: Why don't you put 4 on this side and I can put 4 on this side? [Points to Ed's first peg.]
*Ed*: I'll put 5 on that side.
*Carl*: No.
*Ed*: Ok, but it all should balance; we all know it, cause, see. . . . Now take them [take the blocks out]. See, balance. Now,

> put them back on. [He is referring to putting blocks back under the scale.]
>
> *Ed*: Now you leave it. [He wants Carl to leave his weights alone while he changes his.]
>
> *Carl*: I'll put one.
>
> *Ed*: Uh-huh. Hey. [It didn't balance.] I have five—1, 2, 3, 4, 5.
>
> *Carl*: 1, 2, 3, 4, 5. [Both count their weights on the pegs at the same time.] And let's put the rest [of the weights] on the end [the last peg].
>
> Ed nonverbally complies.
>
> *Ed*: I got it. [He removes block to see if it balances; and he is predicting it will balance.]
>
> *Carl*: Hey [it balances]. (Marquis & Cooper, 1982, Table 2)

This is a creative problem-solving task. At the beginning, neither child has the information or the basic principles required by the task. Through experimentation they gather information and stimulate each other to think about solutions to the problem. The insights and suggestions of both members are part of the success of the pair. In other words, the group is somehow greater than the sum of its parts.

One of the serious criticisms of curriculum in today's schools is the failure to provide experiences with creative problem solving—experiences such as Ed and Carl had. The problems faced by adults in work and social settings clearly require creative problem solving, yet few adults have skills in this area. The recent wave of educational reform generated ten major reports on the ills of education in 1983. Among these reports are *A Nation at Risk*, issued by the National Commission on Excellence in Education (1983), and John Goodlad's *A Place Called School* (1984). In his review of these reports, Kirst (1984) finds that they all agree that the secondary-school curriculum must be refocused as a necessary step toward building the higher order skills of analysis and critical reasoning (pp. 17, 18).

Scientists, science educators, mathematicians, and math educators also agree that curricula must be revised to give students more of a chance to learn problem solving and to see how science and mathematics can be used in everyday applications. The National Council for Teachers of Mathematics (1980) has recommended more emphasis on problem solving and a parallel shift away from excessive drill and practice. Science activities that are concrete and feature practical applications are seen as one of the best ways to teach the general problem-solving skills of recognizing problems, developing procedures for addressing them, and recognizing, evaluating, and applying solutions (Walton, 1983).

In American society, where so much emphasis is placed on individual achievement, it has to be clearly pointed out that creative problem solving is often better done by groups than by an individual working alone. For many years business consultants and educators have used the demonstrations developed by Jay Hall (1971) to teach the simple lesson that groups are superior to individuals in creative problem solving. Hall uses tasks involving problems of survival for a hypothetical group. One activity, for example, is called Lost on the Moon. The group must pull together the creative insights and knowledge of individual members to rank objects in the order of their importance for the group's survival. In these demonstrations it usually turns out that the group score on the task is superior to that of any individual in the group.

Students have much to gain from participating in creative group problem solving. They learn from each other; they are stimulated to carry out higher order thinking; and they experience an authentic intellectual pride of craft when the product is more than what any single member could create.

## Oral Language Proficiency

Cooperative tasks are an excellent tool for still one more cognitive teaching goal—the learning of language and the improvement of oral communication. In any language learning setting, in bilingual classrooms, and for students of any age who need to improve skills in oral communication, active practice is essential. Recitation and drill are of limited effectiveness, producing much less active practice than group exercises where students talk with each other.

Specialists in language learning argue, for example, that there is too much reliance on pattern drills in the English as a

Second Language approach. Children learn language by using it in a more natural, meaningful context. If the instructor of a classroom where children need to increase oral proficiency in English sets up a series of tasks that stimulate children to talk to each other, using new vocabulary associated with an interesting task, the possibilities for active language learning can be greatly enhanced.

The very same proposition applies to teaching foreign languages in secondary school and to speech classes where the instructor is trying to increase skills in oral communication. Compare the traditional approach of having one student stand up and make a presentation to the class with setting up small groups where each member is responsible for communicating a key part of the task. If the group must understand what each member has to say in order to accomplish the goal, they will ask questions and force the presenter to be a clear communicator. The group method will provide far more active and relevant practice than having students take turns making speeches to the whole class.

## SOCIAL GOALS

Social research has gathered impressive evidence to show that when people work together for group goals, there are a number of desirable effects on people's feelings for one another. When members of a group engage in cooperative tasks, they are more likely to form friendly ties, to trust each other, and to influence each other than when the task stimulates competition among members (Deutsch, 1968).

### Positive Intergroup Relations

Cooperative groups and teams are particularly beneficial in developing harmonious interracial relations in desegregated classrooms. Slavin (1983) reviewed fourteen cooperative classroom experiments where groups were ethnically and/or racially mixed. In eleven of these studies there were significantly more friendship choices across racial and ethnic lines among those students who had worked in cooperative, interracial groups than among students who had not had this opportunity. Particularly striking are the results of Slavin's team method (1983, p. 13), where interracial groups are given a group score for the overall score achieved by combining test scores of individual members of the team. In his recent book on cooperative learning, Slavin concludes that it is high-quality positive interpersonal interaction that leads to interpersonal attraction; through interaction individuals perceive underlying similarities across racial lines (Slavin, 1983, Chapter 4). Cooperative goals or group rewards help to produce this deeper level of interaction, interaction that is not usually available in desegregated classrooms.

It is true that an instructor is more likely to produce positive intergroup relations with cooperative groups than with a competitive or individualized reward system. Yet even under cooperative conditions, groups can fail to "mesh" and to achieve a unified "we" feeling. Interpersonal relations can at times be the opposite of harmonious; certain individuals can completely dominate the interaction of the group. To obtain the benefits of cooperation, it is necessary to prepare the students for the cooperative experience. Researchers and educators who work with cooperative classroom groups (including Slavin) have developed ways to train students for the experience of groupwork.

## Socializing Students for Adult Roles

Of all the educators who have written about the favorable effects of small groups in the classroom, only the Sharans (1976) point out that when the teacher delegates authority to a student group and allows that group to make decisions as to how it will proceed on its task, there is a special socializing effect. The Sharans argue that having students experience making decisions on their own rather than telling them exactly what to do will have a desirable political socializing effect on them. They will have more of a sense of control of their own environment, and they will learn how to be active citizens (in a collective rather than in an individualistic sense). This constitutes an antidote to methods of classroom organization where the teacher does all the directing and tells others what to do while the student plays a passive role.

Another way in which groups socialize students for adult roles is by teaching them how to carry on a rational, organized discussion and how to plan and carry out a task as a result of that discussion. This is a set of skills that adults frequently lack; they do not know how to listen to others or how to work with other people's ideas; they are often more concerned with dominating the discourse than with participating. In so many aspects of adult work and organizational life, these skills are critical, yet we rarely teach them in formal education.

## SOLVING COMMON CLASSROOM PROBLEMS

### Increasing Time on Task

Research has led many schools to become concerned with how much time children are actually spending on learning tasks. The issue is important because of the frequently observed relationship between the amount of time children spend in classroom learning activities and their score on achievement tests.

One of the major ways that children lose time on task is through the use of seatwork techniques. The *Beginning Teacher Evaluation Study*, a monumental work of classroom observation and achievement testing, revealed that, on the average, students observed in second and fifth grades spent at least 60 percent of their time doing seatwork (Berliner et al., 1978). For over half the time during reading and mathematics, the students worked on their own, with no instructional guidance. The amount of time children were on task in these self-paced settings was markedly lower than in other classroom settings.

This means that students are often doing something other than their assigned work when they are left to their own devices—and the students observed in the *Beginning Teacher* study were the students who needed to work hard; they were achieving in the 30–60th percentile on standardized tests. Furthermore, regardless of the achievement level of the students in the fall, this study found strong relationships between time on task and achievement test scores in the spring.

Studies of seatwork consistently find this method of instruction has higher rates of disengagement than whole-class instruction. Although seatwork can be supervised effectively, this is frequently not the case. Students often find seatwork assignments meaningless and confusing; they may lack the resources to complete the task properly. In a study of Title I schools (Anderson, 1982), young children were interviewed about what they thought they were doing during seatwork. Many did not understand the purpose of the assignment; "getting it done" was what many students, both high and low achievers, seemed to see as the main reason for doing the task. Of these students, about 30 percent (all of whom were low achievers) apparently did not expect their assignments to make any sense.

Choosing a method of classroom organization that leaves students who rarely succeed in schoolwork quite alone may indeed be the root cause of their disengagement in seatwork settings. These students are receiving very little information on the purpose of their assignment, on how to complete it successfully, on how well they are doing, or on how they could be more successful. The tasks themselves are rarely sufficiently interesting to hold the students' attention. Students drift off task simply because there is nothing to compel them to stay with it except the teacher's command to "get the job done."

Groupwork will usually produce more active, engaged, task-oriented behavior than seatwork. The interactive student situation provides more feedback to the struggling student. Interaction provides more opportunities for active rehearsal of new concepts for students of all achievement levels. Students who cannot read or who do not understand the instructions can receive help from their peers (as in the case of Geraldo). If the group is held accountable for its work, there will be strong group forces that will prevent members from drifting off task. Finally, peer interaction, in and of itself, is enormously engaging and interesting to students. All these factors help to account for research findings such as that of Ahmadjian (1980), who studied low-achieving students in fifth- and sixth-grade classrooms. She found dramatically increased rates of time on task for these students doing groupwork as compared to seat-work.

From the teacher's point of view, groupwork solves two common discipline problems. It helps with the problem of the low-achieving student who is often found doing anything but what he or she is supposed to be doing. Moreover, it helps to solve the problem of what the rest of the class should be doing while the teacher works intensively with one group. The most typical strategy is to have the rest of the students working with pencil and paper at their seats. However, this produces all kinds of discipline problems. If the rest of the class has been trained to work independently in groups, the teacher will be free to give direct instruction to one small group.

## Managing Academic Heterogeneity

Many teachers are faced with students who possess a wide range of academic and linguistic skills in their classes. This is particularly characteristic of schools serving students from lower socioeconomic backgrounds. In many areas of the United States there are classrooms with students who have wide vari-ability in English proficiency. As every teacher knows, this cre-ates tremendous problems. What level of instruction is appropriate? Should students who lack prerequisite academic and English skills be given the same assignment as everyone else, even though they are bound to fail? What should the teacher do with the students who are operating at grade level while giving much-needed attention to students who are so far behind?

The most commonly attempted methods of solving these dilemmas are ability grouping and individualized seatwork. But there is no evidence that ability grouping, particularly for those in low-ability groups, is effective (Hallinan, 1984), and the problems with giving seatwork assignments to students who are operating below grade level have already been emphasized.

An alternative strategy is the use of heterogeneous groups that are trained to use their members as resources. If two students in the group can read, then they can read the instructions to others. If the group problem requires subtraction, and only one student knows how to do subtraction, then that student may be able to show the others how to do it. If several group members speak only Spanish or only English and one student is fully bilingual, then the bilingual student can serve as interpreter between the English- and Spanish-speaking students.

This format allows the teacher to challenge the students intellectually rather than teach down to the lowest common denominator. If each group member is required to turn out a product demonstrating understanding but is allowed to use resources in the group to achieve that understanding, the student with weak academic skills will not sit back and go along with the group. If the task is challenging and interesting, he or she will become actively engaged and will demand assistance and explanation. For students more advanced in academic skills, the act of explaining to others represents one of the finest ways to solidify their own learning.

In review, if students are properly prepared, heterogeneous groups can represent a solution to one of the most persistent problems of classroom teaching. If students are able to use each other as resources, everyone can be exposed to grade-level curriculum and even more challenging material. Lack of skills in reading, writing, and computation need not bar students from exposure to lessons requiring conceptualization. At the same time, these students can develop their basic skills with assistance from their classmates.

# 3 The Dilemma of Groupwork

A very common problem in groupwork can be illustrated by a visit to a hypothetical classroom, in this case that of Ms. Todd, who is making her first attempt at using groupwork in her class. Ms. Todd has decided that she has been doing too much of the talking in class and that students should have the opportunity for more participation. She has given her fifth-grade class a group assignment in social studies based on a chapter from the textbook along with the comprehension questions provided in the teacher's manual. The class has supposedly already read this chapter. Each group has been told that they are expected to answer the questions as a group. At the end of the period each group is to hand in one set of answers that represents the group's opinion. Ms. Todd was afraid that if she tried to compose the groups, the students would be upset at being separated from their friends. Therefore she has told them that they must find a group of four with whom they would like to work.

We look in on the classroom ten minutes into the period and find the work under way: There is a constructive buzz of voices as students bend to their task. Everything appears to be going very well indeed, although as we look around we realize that the groups have segregated themselves so that they are either all boy or all girl. Wait a minute! What is going on in the group by the window? As we quietly move nearer we can see that two of the four students have their heads together over the book. One has the answer paper and the other is leafing through the chapter looking for the answer. The other two members of the group, however, are not working on this task at all. One seems to be finishing a math assignment, and the other is gazing dreamily out the window.

And look at that other group in the back of the room! Did you hear what they said? One girl just told the others that she didn't have time to read the chapter, so she won't be much help. Another is saying to the group, "Look, Susanna is the only one who gets A's in social studies, so we should only put down what she thinks. Susanna, you tell us the answers, and I'll write them down for you."

In a third group of boys over by the door, Rick Williams is acting like a regular Mr. Take-Charge. He is telling everyone where to look things up, and then when they come up with an answer, he always thinks he has a better idea. What's worse—even when his ideas are clearly wrong, the group goes along with him.

There are just three black students in this otherwise all-white classroom (the school is part of a small voluntary deseg-regation program). How are they doing in the groupwork scene? Look, two of them are not saying very much in their groups. They have the book open and look interested, but no one in the group is paying any attention to them.

And how is poor little Annie doing? No one chose Annie as a group member because she doesn't have any friends in the class. Ms. Todd whispers to us that she had to "persuade" one of the groups to accept Annie as a member and that it was em-barrassing. Annie, at the moment we observe, has her head on her arms; her eyes are closed.

Now things are getting a little out of hand. In still another group two boys are just about to come to blows over what is the right answer. They really don't seem so concerned over social studies as they are over who is going to be boss. Those two are friends, but they fight all the time. At least they are arguing over the assignment, which is better than one of the other groups of boys currently engaged in an arm-wrestling contest. That is not too surprising, considering that Jimmy is the ring-leader; Jimmy can only read at the third-grade level and just hates social studies.

"Let's have a little order in here!" pleads Ms. Todd, who

has been moving around the room and has seen what is going on. "Five more minutes," she calls out—even though the period is only half over. We decide we had better leave. Ms. Todd looks uncomfortable with having visitors, and she is not pleased with what is happening.

Why were the results of Ms. Todd's experiment so dismaying? This classroom scene raises many issues about what goes on inside small groups. Why do the sexes voluntarily segregate themselves? Why do the students allow one member of the group to do all the work and make all the decisions? It makes some sense in Susanna's case, because she really is a top-notch student, but look at Rick's group. They are going along with Rick's ideas even when they must know he is wrong—he just talks more loudly than the others. In the cases of Rick, Jimmy (the classroom troublemaker and schoolyard hero), the two students who are arguing foolishly just to see whose opinion will carry the day, and unpopular little Annie, it is almost as if the pecking order of student play and friendship groups has invaded the classroom groups. And why aren't the students nicer to each other? Why aren't they aware of how those two black students must feel about having no chance to talk? And why don't they see that Annie is on the verge of tears?

One thing is clear: What we have seen helps to explain why one rarely sees groupwork in either elementary or secondary school. The teacher who has no more tools for the planning of groupwork than an initial attraction to an idea of groupwork as a democratic and creative setting for learning is likely to run into trouble in trying out the new methods. Although the results are unlikely to be as consistently disappointing as in Ms. Todd's class, careful observation of any class working under her form of grouping and task instruction will reveal patterns of undesirable domination on the part of some students and nonparticipation and withdrawal on the part of others. In addition, there appear to be both disciplinary and motivational problems that are not characteristic of Ms. Todd's class when she uses her more traditional methods of whole class presentation or well-supervised seatwork.

Some of these disciplinary and motivational problems are

closely related to our initial observations of domination and lack of participation. Some are related to Ms. Todd's failure to select and define a more suitable task for the groupwork setting and her failure to prepare the students for the skills they will need for groupwork. This chapter focuses on the problems of unequal participation and undesirable domination of groups by certain students.

Let us imagine that Ms. Todd persists beyond the first trial and in her second attempt tries to compose groups so that students of more similar abilities are placed together. She reasons that one student who gets much better grades won't take over and do all the work. Furthermore, this arrangement has the added advantage of separating friends who play rather than work, spares her the problem of Annie the social isolate, and desegregates the sexes.

As she walks around the room and listens carefully to what is happening in each group, she finds that although the discipline problem is much improved, in most of her groups one student is doing far more talking and deciding than anyone else, and at least one student is saying practically nothing. Again two of the three black students are quiet members of their respective groups. In at least one of the groups she observes, there is a real struggle going on as to whose opinion will be adopted by the group. Their talk is not an intellectual discussion about the meaning of the chapter but an interpersonal conflict over who is going to be the leader of the group.

What is the matter? Are the students just too immature to work in groups? The problem is not one of immaturity: Adults working in small groups will also exhibit problems of dominance—they will struggle over leadership in a group and will participate unequally.

## BEHAVIOR OF TASK-ORIENTED GROUPS

Small task groups tend to develop hierarchies where some members are more active and influential than others. This is a *status ordering*—an agreed-upon social ranking where everyone feels that it is better to have a high rank within the status order than a low rank. Group members who have high rank are seen as more competent and as having done more to guide and lead the group.

In the more than 100 four-person groups of schoolchildren I have studied, I have rarely found that each person contributes one-fourth of the speeches on the task. Even among a group of adults who do not know each other and who have been selected for a laboratory study on the basis that they are all male, nineteen or twenty years old, and white, inequalities in interaction and a status order will emerge. After the task is completed, group members are likely to agree that the person who has done the most talking has made the most important contribution to the task and has had the best ideas, while the person who was relatively quiet is seen as having made the least important contribution and is felt to have contributed few good ideas (Berger, Conner, & McKeown, 1969).

## Expert Status

If dominance and inequality emerge in groups with members who are equal in status, then we should not be surprised to find these patterns in classroom groups where students have known each other on an intensive basis in what is often a competitive setting. In the classroom it is impossible to compose groups where all members have equal status. Students generally have an idea of the relative competence of each of their classmates in important subjects like reading and math acquired from listening to their classmates perform, from hearing the teacher's evaluation of that performance, and from finding out each other's marks and grades. They usually can, if asked, place each of their classmates in a rank order of competence in reading and math. This ranking forms an *academic status order* in the classroom.

Students who have high standing in an academic subject are very likely to dominate a group given a task from that subject area—recall Susanna's group in Ms. Todd's class. Susanna was viewed as a very successful student in social studies. People who are seen as knowing more about the specific topic of the group task are very likely to be highly influential in the group. In other words, they are high status individuals.

Expert status is an important idea for the designer of groupwork. If you assign a group a task from regular academic work, the student who is seen as getting the best grades in that subject is likely to dominate the group. Even if you think you have picked group members of similar ability, the students are likely to make very fine distinctions about who is the best student in the small group.

As a teacher you may decide that there is nothing undesirable about experts dominating their groups, as long as they are on the right track on this particular assignment. If they are not, the group may miss the point of the assignment because members are unwilling to argue with the expert. Also, students who feel as if they are distinctly less expert within the group may sit back and play a very passive role, learning little from the experience.

## Academic Status

Now suppose Ms. Todd does not pick a social studies task from the textbook. Suppose she asks her students to play a simple board game called Shoot the Moon. On the board are many different paths to the moon. Depending on which square the playing piece lands on, the group stands to win or lose the number of points printed in each square on the board. A roll of a die determines how many spaces the playing piece advances. The group has only fourteen turns to reach the goal in their rocket ship. For each turn, they must come to agreement as to which way to proceed on the board.

Shoot the Moon is a game requiring no academic skills. There is no rational connection between reading skills and the ability to play Shoot the Moon. Yet the student who is seen as best in reading is very likely to dominate the discussion. And the student who is seen as poor in reading is very likely to be relatively inactive in this game. Reading ability, as perceived by others, is an important kind of academic status. And academic status has the power to spread to new tasks where there is no rational connection between the abilities required by the task and the academic skill making up the status order.

Rosenholtz (1985) demonstrated the power of reading ability to affect the status order in classroom groups playing Shoot the Moon. After she asked fifth- and sixth-grade children to rank each other on how good they were in reading, she composed groups with two classmates who were seen as more able in reading and two who were seen as less able. Those perceived as better readers were more active and influential compared to those seen as less able in reading. Thus reading ability, a kind of academic status, had the power to spread to a task where reading was irrelevant.

Children (and some teachers) see reading ability as an index of something more general than a specific, relatively mechanical skill. Reading ability is used as an index of how smart a student is. Thus good readers expect to be good at a wide range of school tasks, and poor readers expect to do poorly at just as wide a range of schoolwork.

Rank on reading ability is evidently public knowledge in many elementary classrooms. In most of the classrooms studied by Rosenholtz and Wilson (1980) the students were able to rank order each other on reading ability with a high level of agreement. Furthermore, the teacher's ranking was in agreement with the students' ranking. This means that if you are poor reader, it is not only you who expect to do poorly—all your classmates expect you to do poorly as well! It is an unenviable status, particularly when one thinks of how many hours a day you are imprisoned in a situation where no one expects you to perform well. Even in the higher grades where reading is no longer a regular subject of study, students will still show considerable agreement on who in the class is best in schoolwork and who has the most trouble with schoolwork (Hoffman & Cohen, 1972). Just as in the Rosenholtz study described above, Hoffman found that those students who were seen as better in schoolwork tended to be more dominant on a game requiring no academic skill in comparison to those who were seen as less able in schoolwork.

## Peer Status

Returning to Ms. Todd's class for a moment, why did we see some children who had a high social standing among their peers (like Rick and Jimmy) dominate in their groups even though they were not good students? And why was Annie, who had no friends, so inactive in her group? Students create their own status orders as they play with each other at school and outside of school. Those who have a higher social standing have high *peer status* and are likely to dominate classroom groups. Among students, peer status may be based on athletic competence or on attractiveness and popularity. Those with a lower social standing are likely to be less active participants. In this way a group inside a schoolroom can reflect the world of the schoolyard, even though the task is academic and has nothing to do with play.

## Societal Status

Classrooms exhibit one other kind of status that will affect student participation in small groups. In the society at large there are status distinctions made on the basis of social class, race, ethnic group, and sex. These are general social rankings on which most people agree that it is better to be of a higher social class, white, and male than it is to be of a lower social class, black or brown, or female. (At least that is what people believe in many Western societies.)

Just like academic status and peer status, societal status has the power to affect what happens in a small group. Within interracial groups of junior high school boys who played Shoot the Moon, the whites were more likely than blacks to be influential and active (Cohen, 1972). This happened even though the boys did not know each other and saw themselves as equally good students in school. Likewise, other studies have found that men are more often dominant than women in mixed-sex groups; and Anglos are more often dominant than Mexican-Americans who have an ethnically distinctive appearance (Rosenholtz & Cohen, 1985).

Why do these status differences affect participation? Why should some students have so much influence on tasks where they have no special competence? Why should new groups working on new tasks reflect preexisting status orders among the students? In order to modify this process, the teacher needs to understand more about how and why it operates.

## EXPECTATIONS AND THE SELF-FULFILLING PROPHECY

Basic to our understanding of the way in which the process operates is the idea of a *status characteristic*. A status characteristic is an agreed-upon social ranking where everyone feels it is better to have a high rank than a low rank. Examples of status characteristics are race, social class, sex, reading ability, and attractiveness.

Attached to these status characteristics are general expectations for competence. High status individuals are expected to be more competent than low status individuals across a wide range of tasks that are viewed as important. When a teacher assigns a task to a group of students, some of whom are higher and some lower on any of the status characteristics described above, these general expectations come into play. They cause a kind of self-fulfilling prophecy to take place in which those who are higher status come to hold high rank in the status order that emerges from the group interaction. Those who hold lower status come to hold a low rank on that same status order.

From the start of the group's interaction, high status students are expected to be more competent at the new assignment; moreover, these students also expect themselves to be more competent. This is due to the operation of general expectations for competence described above. Thus they are very likely to start participating right away.

Low status students, who are not expected to make an important contribution and who share the group's evaluation of themselves, are unlikely to say much of anything. As high status students continue to talk, others tend to address their remarks to them, and one of them rapidly becomes the most influential person in the group. By the end of the interaction, this person is likely to be viewed by group members as having made the most important contribution to the group's performance. Thus the status order that emerges from the group assignment is very much like the initial differences in status with which the group started.

Returning to Shoot the Moon for a moment, when interracial groups knew nothing about each other than differences in race, whites were more likely to be active and influential than blacks (Cohen, 1972). In this case, the group used race as a basis for forming expectations for competence on the game. Since in our culture blacks are generally expected to be less competent on intellectual tasks than whites, these racist expectations came into play in the innocent game of Shoot the Moon. Once this had happened, it was very likely that the whites would talk more and become more influential in group decision making than the blacks.

In accordance with Expectation States Theory (Berger, Rosenholtz, & Zelditch, 1980), the same thing happened in the Rosenholtz groups playing Shoot the Moon. Here the students used information they had about each other's standing on the academic status characteristic of reading ability to organize their expectations for competence on the new game of Shoot the Moon. Group interaction turned out to mirror initial differences in reading ability.

In the classes that Rosenholtz studied, peer status was closely related to academic status so that those students who were seen as influential in the informal social relations between classmates tended to be the same students who were seen as best in schoolwork. In other classrooms, students like Jimmy in Ms. Todd's class will have high peer status but low academic status. Students with high peer status will have the same effect on a classroom group as students with high academic status; in either case they are likely to be more active and influential than students with either low peer status (like Annie) or low academic status.

A note of caution is necessary. The operation of expectations based on status does not result in the domination by high status children of every group in the classroom. Although research finds that, on the whole, high status persons are more active and influential than low status persons, in the case of particular groups, some low status members are more influential than high status members. There are two other factors that help to account for what happens in a particular task group. These are the nature of the task, and who participates frequently at the beginning of the session.

Studies of small-group interaction almost always conclude that some of the patterns of behavior observed are a function of the peculiarities of the task that has been selected. The same holds true of classrooms. Suppose that you introduce a science task in which the group is asked to do observations of a live meal worm. Some students will be fascinated with touching and holding the worm, while others will be squeamish. Those who are fascinated are likely to be more active and influential than those who are squeamish. This ordering of behavior is linked to the peculiar nature of this task and may have nothing to do with the standing of the children on any of the status characteristics we have discussed. The nature of the task can also affect the total amount of interaction in the group. Some classroom tasks are intrinsically interesting and provoke a high level of interaction while others are boring and produce only desultory talk. Still other classroom tasks may be carried out nonverbally, by manipulating the material or by communicating through writing. Such tasks will have a low level of verbal interaction, but a high level of other kinds of communication.

In addition to differences stemming from the nature of the task, studies of groups show that members who start talking right away, regardless of their status, are likely to become influential. Suppose Annie had been given the task of handing out the materials to the group. She might have had an advance look at these materials and so might have been able to explain what was to be done with them. Just such an event can change what happens in a particular group quite radically. Because the group would need to turn to her from the beginning to find out more about the materials, Annie might have become quite active and influential in that particular group.

## EDUCATIONAL DISADVANTAGES OF DOMINANCE AND INEQUALITY

Why should a teacher be so concerned about patterns of unequal interaction in the classroom? After all, not all children have equal ability, so it is only to be expected that those who get better grades will tend to dominate classroom groups. It is also only natural that those who are social leaders among the children will be looked up to, even in the classroom setting.

There are several good answers to this. The first has to do with learning. If you design a good groupwork task, learning emerges from the chance to talk, interact, and contribute to the group discussion. Those who do not participate because they are of low status will learn less than they might have if they had interacted more. In addition, those who are of high status will have more access to the interaction and will therefore learn more. It is a case of the "rich getting richer" in the classroom setting. In classroom research on a curriculum using learning centers, children who talked and worked together more showed higher gains on their test scores than children who talked and worked together less. Furthermore, children who had high peer and academic status did much more talking and working together than those who had lower peer and academic status (Cohen, 1984). Thus the operation of status can impair the learning of low status students in the groupwork setting.

The second answer to the question has to do with the issue of equity. Most teachers want classrooms to offer children equal chances to succeed in school, regardless of race, sex, or socioeconomic background. They also hope that the classroom will be a setting where children who have different societal statuses will meet each other and learn that stereotypical and prejudicial beliefs held by society are not true. Teachers want children of different statuses to learn to treat each other as individuals rather than as members of particular social groups.

If status characteristics are allowed to operate unchecked in the classroom, the interaction of the children will only reinforce the prejudices they entered school with. For example, if the black children in a classroom who come from poorer homes consistently come to be viewed as less competent in group-work, racist beliefs about the relative incompetence of blacks will only be reinforced. If the leadership position in groups always falls to boys, it will reinforce the cultural belief that "girls can't be leaders."

This problem of reinforcement of stereotypes is not avoided by using only whole-group instruction or supervised ability groups. If the children have very little chance to interact with each other, cultural prejudices will have no opportunity to be challenged. Group interaction offers a *chance* to attack these prejudices, but the teacher must do more than simply assign groupwork tasks.

The third answer to the question of why unequal interaction should be a matter of concern has to do with the intellectual quality of group performance. In order to get the best possible group product, it is critical that each member have an equal opportunity to contribute. If some members are hesitant to speak up even though they have much better ideas, the intellectual quality of the group's performance suffers. Subservience to a loud-talking and dominant peer is not what teachers have in mind when they set a group discussion task. When two members of a group engage in a struggle over which one will be dominant, the quality of the performance almost always suffers. Thus the operation of status within groups is often inconsistent with high-quality group performance.

What is the ideal pattern of group interaction in an educational setting? Over a series of groupwork assignments one would expect different children to play influential roles depending on their ability, interest, and expertise; the nature of the task; and a number of chance factors. This is not to say that there is no such thing as differences in ability to contribute to tasks. Each task requires different abilities, and it would seem desirable for those who are strong in these abilities or who are expert in a particular topic to do more talking and explaining and to be viewed as more competent. These inequalities become a problem, however, when a child's status on a rank order that has nothing to do with the task becomes the basis for dominance in the group. For example, we can all recognize that ability in reading is a valuable skill and that readers can make an important contribution to a group task where some children have difficulty with reading. This becomes a problem when the good reader is assumed to be better at everything and thus dominates all aspects of groupwork. When ability in one area is used as an index of general intelligence and classroom competence, you are dealing with a status problem.

This chapter has posed a dilemma: While groupwork is attractive for sound educational reasons, it can activate status problems within small groups. Chapters 4, 5, and especially 8 contain some specific suggestions about how to gain the advantages of groupwork without its drawbacks.

# 4 Preparing Students for Cooperation

The first step in introducing groupwork to a classroom is to prepare students for cooperative work situations. It is a great mistake to assume that children (or adults) know how to work with each other in a constructive collegial fashion. The chances are that they have not had previous successful experiences in cooperative tasks, working with people who are not personal friends or family members. They may never have experienced small formal-discussion groups or collective decision-making groups. The cooperative experience they have had may be limited to team sports, but roles in sports are closely guided by the rules of the game, and the coach or referee has the final word.

Students must be prepared for cooperation so that they know how to behave in the groupwork situation without direct supervision. It is necessary to introduce new cooperative behaviors in a training program. The goal of the training program is the construction of new norms.

A *norm* is a rule for how one ought to behave. When an individual comes to feel that he or she ought to behave in this new way, the norm has become *internalized*. Sometimes norms are written rules, and sometimes people just act as if everyone were expected to behave in this way.

The students must internalize the norms for working in a group. When they have, not only will they behave according to the new norms, but they will enforce rules on other group members. In cooperative learning settings, even very young students can be heard lecturing to other members of the group on how they ought to be behaving. When you hear students reminding others of how they should behave, you know that the norm you have introduced has become internalized.

Teachers have far more power than they realize in constructing new norms for classroom behavior. Recall how the beginning teacher is told to lay down the law on the first day of class. "Be even stricter on the first day than you will actually be later on" is common advice from the experienced teacher. The teacher is setting the norms for this particular classroom and informing the students that regardless of what they may have "gotten away with" in someone else's classroom, the written and unwritten rules for this classroom are different and will be enforced.

The norms of traditional classrooms include: Do your own work and don't pay attention to what other students are doing; never give or ask for advice from a fellow student while doing an assignment in class; pay attention to what the teacher is saying and doing and not to anything else; eyes front and be quiet. When dealing with younger students, teachers constantly reinforce these norms through repetition, reward, and punishment. By the time students are in high school, norms have become internalized to such an extent that students are quite unconscious of why they behave in class the way they do.

Assigning group tasks involves a major change in traditional classroom norms. Now the student is supposed to depend on other students. Now students are responsible not only for their own behavior but for group behavior and for the product of group efforts. Instead of listening to the teacher, they must learn to listen to other students. In order for the group to work smoothly they must learn to ask for other people's opinions, to give other people a chance to talk, and to make brief, sensible contributions to the group effort. These are examples of new norms that are useful to teach before the start of groupwork.

## TRAINING FOR COOPERATION

Students need to understand your purposes in introducing small groups and why groupwork skills are important. I was amazed to discover that some children in the sixth grade do not realize that adult life calls for working with people who are not close friends. Students in one class called a halt to the training program; they felt that the instructors were trying to force them to be friends with classmates assigned to their group. When it was explained to them that in the work world many important tasks are accomplished in small groups of people who are not personal friends, such as research teams, fire-fighting personnel, nursing teams, committees, construction crews, and the like, they were still so doubtful that we had them ask their parents if this were true. Once their parents concurred that this is indeed how adults work, the students accepted membership in groups composed by the teacher.

Preparing students for cooperative groups requires you to decide which norms and which skills will be needed for the groupwork setting you have in mind. These norms and skills are best taught through exercises and games. People rarely learn new behaviors or convictions about how one ought to behave through lecture or general group discussion alone.

The remainder of this chapter will provide the principles for your design of a training program. Appendix A at the back of the book contains detailed instructions for a number of games and exercises that have worked very well for many teachers. What if none of these particular activities exactly fits the skills and norms needed for your training program? Once you see the principles on which they are based, you can adapt the activities described or make up some of your own.

One note of caution about the games and exercises: Don't judge their suitability for your class by whether or not they seem too easy for your students. The point of the activities is for students to learn how to work together. The tasks themselves are just a vehicle for new skills and norms, not an end in themselves. They should not be too complex; otherwise students will be distracted from group processes and will become too involved in the activity for its own sake. In each case, the key to learning lies in the combination of the experience and the discussion that follows the game. The teacher must assist the class in reflecting on important features of what has happened and in developing key insights about the relevance of this experience to the forthcoming groupwork.

## Learning to Be Responsive to the Needs of the Group

Responsiveness to the needs of the group is a skill required of any kind of cooperative task. If students are oblivious to the problems experienced by peers, the group will not function properly, the group product will be inferior, and the interaction will not provide access to learning for all its members. Students need to learn how to take the part of other members of the group and to feel responsible for helping them for the sake of the group product.

One of the best ways to teach this skill is with a group exercise called Broken Circles. It was developed by anthropologists Nancy Graves and Ted Graves from a classic exercise called the Broken Squares problem (Pfeiffer & Jones, 1970). In Broken Circles a puzzle cannot be satisfactorily solved unless group members become aware of problems being experienced by others and are willing to give away their pieces of the puzzle in order to attain the group goal.

Each member of the group is given an envelope containing pieces of cardboard. The task of each group is to form circles of equal size. The task is not completed until each individual has before him or her a perfect circle of the same size as that formed by others in the group. There are specific limitations on the interaction: No speaking is allowed. Members may not ask for or take pieces from other persons. They may only give fellow members pieces that they may need. Detailed directions for this exercise and follow-up discussion suggestions appear in Appendix A.

The challenge lies in the fact that exchange of pieces must take place between members before the goal is achieved. For all but the easiest version of this exercise, some of the envelopes given to each group contain pieces that will produce a circle without exchange. However, if the person who receives such an envelope is unwilling to break up his solution and share with others, the group will not be able to solve the problem. What often happens in a group is that one of the more competitive members quickly finishes a complete shape and then impatiently waits for the others to solve their problem, gazing around the room and paying no attention to the struggles of other members of the group—quite unaware that he or she is the cause of the group failure.

By eliciting ideas during the postgame discussion of what made for successful or unsuccessful cooperation in the group, you can help the students gain key insights about sensitivity to needs of others and sharing. Ask them how they could have cooperated more fully. This task is an excellent analog to many cooperative tasks; the individual must be concerned with giving rather than with taking or showing off individual achievement.

Do not lecture students on what they are supposed to learn from the experience. Allow them to arrive at conclusions through your questions and the discussion that follows. Then, when they have been able to develop the important insights, you can point out how cooperation in this situation relates to cooperation in the planned groupwork. Education is not magic—always make the connection between the new behaviors and the situation when you want the students to use their new awareness or skills.

### Follow-up experiences

Very often it is necessary to design a follow-up experience if the groups are exhibiting problems in being responsive and sharing. An advanced version of Broken Circles (see Appendix A) allows the same class to do the exercise at a later time. Or you can provide a supplementary experience with sharing pieces of a jigsaw puzzle, as also described in Appendix A.

Other activities that can be used to teach the same lesson include a workout with a large medicine ball where the group is given the task of keeping the huge ball in the air and bouncing for so many minutes. Here, too, the success of the group will depend on everyone's efforts. Creating a mural together or other joint artwork can teach or review the very same point about cooperation. As with the first activity, it should be followed by a discussion where the students have a chance to draw the connections between cooperation demanded by the exercise and their own behavior in the groupwork setting.

## Teaching Specific Cooperative Behaviors

Your training program should deal with specific behaviors that are required by the groupwork setting you have in mind. Start by analyzing your groupwork task. Will it be a small discussion group where everyone must come to consensus? Will it be a working group where students help each other in a collegial fashion but are responsible for their own product, such as a completed worksheet or laboratory report? Will the task be a purely verbal one involving values and opinions, or will the task involve students showing each other how things work with manipulative materials? Will the task involve creative problem solving in a situation where there are clearly better and worse answers?

Upon close analysis, it turns out that different groupwork tasks require different cooperative behaviors. To illustrate, let me contrast the behaviors called for in two groupwork settings that I have studied extensively—learning centers and small discussion groups. In the learning center format, the instructor sets up different tasks in various stations in the classroom. These might be science experiments, manipulative math problems, or map making in social studies. Tasks are typically multimedia and call for a variety of problem-solving behaviors, with more than one way to solve each part of the problem. There are clear standards by which one can judge the productions of the students as more or less successful. Students are expected to work together to help others at their center; at the same time they are expected to turn out individual worksheets or products that the teacher can examine and use as a basis for individual evaluation.

A key behavior for learning centers is helping other students. Helping others is not as simple as it sounds; the most common response is to help by doing the task for the other person rather than helping people to do things for themselves. Students also need encouragement in asking each other questions in this setting. They need to realize that this is a legitimate and recommended behavior at learning centers. Furthermore, they need to know how to answer each other's questions; instead of telling the "right answer," students must learn how to give a full explanation. In this collegial situation there is a distinction between the students' finding out what others think and deciding for themselves what they are going to include in their own final production. Students need to be encouraged to consult with others but make up their own minds in creating their individual product. Finally, if students are to have a productive interchange at the learning center, they will need some practice in listening behavior. Both the question asker and the answerer must know how to listen carefully.

Younger children often need special practice in using language to give explanations. Although many questions concerning this type of manipulative task can be answered by physical demonstration with materials, nonverbal communication is too confining as the only method of communication. Younger children need practice in *telling how* as well as in *showing how* things can be done. Finally, younger children need to learn new ways in which to be polite in a collegial setting; when someone gives you assistance, you should thank them or show your appreciation in some way.

Required behaviors for small discussion groups differ in some dramatic ways from those required by learning centers. Here the task is one of verbal exchange as well as the requirement that the group reach some kind of a consensus. For example, you might ask the groups to arrive at some interpretation of literature or drama, solve a word problem in mathematics, use the assigned readings to answer a discussion question, apply what they have learned about nutrition to plan a meal, create a pantomime or role play illustrating an idea, create a five-minute conversation using new words in a foreign-language class, improve the grammar and sentence structure of a composition written by a classmate, or arrive at a solution of a social or political problem.

The basic set of required behaviors includes, at minimum, the norms that everyone should contribute and that no one person should dominate the group. In addition, discussion requires listening skills. There is a tendency for members to be so concerned about saying their piece that they don't listen to what someone has just said. Not only do people have to listen to each other, but they need to learn to think about what the other person has said. Lack of listening and reflection on what others have said results in a disconnected discussion and often in a failure to reach consensus.

While older students need to learn to be concise in giving their ideas, younger students should learn to give reasons for their ideas. If the group is asked to come to consensus, then students will have to learn how to pull ideas together and to find out if the group is ready to decide what to do. Youngsters are typically unaware that coming to a collective decision involves some procedural discussion about how and when the group will narrow down to a decision. This is evidently learned in formal club and committee settings; even high school students do not engage in as much procedural talk as adults. A comparison of behaviors needed in the two settings is summarized in Figure 4.1.

### Use of social learning principles

Detailed instructions for training exercises designed to teach behaviors such as those listed in Figure 4.1 are included in Appendix A. However, if you grasp the simple principles

FIGURE 4.1: Student Behaviors Required in Learning Centers and Discussion Groups

| *Learning Centers* | *Discussion Groups* |
|---|---|
| Asking questions | Asking for others' opinions |
| Listening | Listening |
| Helping others | Reflecting on what has been |
| Helping students do things for | said |
| themselves | Being concise |
| Showing others how to do things | Giving reasons for ideas |
| Explaining by telling how and why | Allowing everyone to |
| Finding out what others think | contribute |
| Making up his/her own mind | Pulling ideas together |
|  | Finding out if group is |
|  | ready to make decision |

behind the construction of these exercises you can create training experiences for these and for any other skills you decide are important for the groupwork you have chosen.

Bandura (1969) and others have developed some relatively simple principles of social learning through extensive experimentation. These are extraordinarily useful whenever one is introducing new behaviors to children or adults. These principles may be summarized as follows:

1. New behaviors must be labeled and discussed.
2. Students must learn to recognize when new behaviors occur.
3. Students must be able to use labels and discuss behavior in an objective way.
4. Students must have a chance to practice new behaviors.
5. New behaviors should be reinforced when they occur.

Any training exercise you develop should meet the requirements of these five principles. If you take the trouble to do so, you will have a very good chance of seeing the students make frequent and correct use of their new skills. Actually, they are learning more than the new behaviors; they are learning that these are effective ways of behaving if they want a good group product. Furthermore, they are learning that these are desirable and preferable ways of behaving in groupwork situations. In sociological terms, they will be willing to enforce these new norms on their peers in the group.

Let me illustrate the use of these five principles in an exercise called "Master Designer," which is described in detail in Appendix A. Master Designer teaches elementary-school students three new behaviors for their work in groups at learning centers. The game requires a set of seven geometric shapes (illustrated in Appendix A). Each of the four players in a group needs a complete set. The fifth member of the group is the observer. One player takes the role of master designer, who creates a design with the shapes. The master designer then must instruct the others as to how to replicate the design without showing it to them. Group members cannot see what the other members are doing, but they may ask questions of the master designer.

The game of Master Designer illustrates three new behaviors. It shows students how to help other students do things for themselves. It illustrates how a group can be dependent on the master designer for explaining how a project should be done. And by virtue of another of its rules—after the master designer has certified a member's design as correct, that person may also help others by explaining how—it shows students that everyone's cooperation can lead to the group's success.

Before the game begins, the teacher introduces the new behaviors and assigns them labels: "Helping Students Do Things for Themselves," "Explaining by Telling How," and "Everybody Helps." These labels should appear on a poster that remains on display for the groupwork that follows training. In accordance with the social learning principles, assigning labels helps to fix the new behaviors in the students' minds; playing the game provides them with a chance to practice the new behaviors. In subsequent rounds another student can take the role of master designer, thus giving others a chance to practice helping others.

The job of the observers is to watch the group and check off every time they see two of the three new behaviors: Explain by Telling How and Everybody Helps. After each round of the game, the observers report how many times they saw the new behaviors. According to principles of social learning, the observer role teaches students to recognize new behaviors when they occur and to discuss them with the correct labels.

It is very important to prepare the observers for their role. You cannot assume that students will automatically be able to recognize the new behaviors you have in mind—the words may have a very different meaning for them than for you. Discussing what the behaviors are and how to look for them is an essential step if everyone is to gain a common awareness of what behaviors you are talking about. When the observers later report what happened in the groups, you have an opportunity to reinforce the new behaviors. In this way the game uses all five of the learning principles listed earlier.

The Four-Stage Rocket exercise (described in Appendix A) embodies the same learning principles. A technique developed by Charlotte Epstein in her book, *Affective Subjects in the Classroom* (1972, pp. 48–57), this exercise for small-group skills has become a general favorite of cooperative-training practitioners. It can be adapted to teach a variety of particular skills needed for different kinds of group tasks. Guess My Rule and training tasks for discussion in Appendix A teach skills needed in learning centers and discussion groups. These exercises are self-explanatory.

### Training during groupwork

During the course of groupwork, you will see some loss of training, some slipping back to old ways. When this happens simply take time to refresh everyone's mind on what important behaviors make for a successful experience. Ask the students if they are having any difficulties in the groups. Can they think of any way to solve these problems? Do they remember some of the new behaviors that might help? Tell the groups to repeat or extend an assignment they have already carried out. Appoint an observer for each group. The groups will work for five minutes while the observer watches for use of specific recommended behaviors. Then stop the groups and allow each group to discuss with their observer what was seen and what can be done to improve the quality of the group process. There is no need at this point to go back to games and exercises that are not directly related to the work at hand. The group itself should have the capacity to be self-critical and to correct its problems.

There are additional skills, especially for group projects, that become more important as groups attempt longer-term, more ambitious projects. Supplementary training can take the same form as the review of basic behaviors just described. Elizabeth Hunter (1972) has developed lists of helping and troublesome behaviors for improving group process skills, which are provided in Appendix A. Use an observer with a scoring sheet while the group repeats or extends an assignment. The observers can report to the class as a whole or to their own groups. This should be followed by a discussion of whether or not the students feel these behaviors are important to group functioning. The students should also discuss alternative strategies of exhibiting helping behaviors and avoiding troublesome behaviors. Simply choose those behaviors from the list you think will be useful for your class; don't feel bound to teach every single one.

## Norms for Equal Participation

Probably the most important rule to teach when training students to discuss, to make decisions, and to do creative problem solving is the norm for equal participation. When students feel that everyone *ought* to have their say and receive a careful hearing, the problems of inequality and dominance discussed in the last chapter can, in part, be solved. As long as group members have internalized this new norm and have acquired some skills for discussion, students with high status are not so likely to dominate the group.

In a laboratory study, Morris (1977) demonstrated the effectiveness of training procedures in preventing unwanted dominance in creative problem-solving groups. The focus of Morris' treatment was on the establishment of special norms for solving problems through group discussion: norms for participation and listening. The students learned that these behaviors would contribute to a successful outcome for the group task.

Although based on a laboratory experiment, Morris' treatment is applicable to the classroom with very little modification. It could be used in conjunction with the Four-Stage Rocket in preparing students for creative problem solving. Here are the guidelines for cooperative problem-solving behavior Morris (1977, p. 63) presented to his subjects:

1. Say your own ideas.
2. Listen to others; give everyone a chance to talk.
3. Ask others for their ideas.
4. Give reasons for your ideas and discuss many different ideas.

In order to train groups to use these norms, Morris gave them a challenging survival problem to solve. This task, adapted from survival problems developed by Jay Hall (1971), is called Shipwreck. It requires the group to imagine it is a crew of a ship sinking near a tropical island. Eight items are available to take with them from the ship. The group is asked to rank order items as to how important each is for the group's survival. This and the other survival problems developed by Hall are excellent for the teaching of creative problem solving because he provides a best ordering of the items prepared by survival experts. Thus the group can come up with better and worse answers to the problem.

After discussing how research has shown that groups do better than individuals on creative problem solving, Morris (1977) introduced the task and told the group that they were going to work as a team and that they would be evaluated on how well they worked together. Lastly, he explained the four behaviors that make a good team effort.

In order to teach the group to be self-critical, he interrupted them after they had arranged four items to evaluate group process. He used the following discussion questions:

1. Is everyone talking?
2. Are you listening to each other?
3. Are you asking questions? What could you ask to find out someone's ideas?
4. Are you giving reasons for ideas and getting out different ideas? What could you ask if you wanted to find out someone's reason for a suggestion? (Morris, 1977, p. 157)

He then allowed them to finish the task and presented them with another similar survival problem. This research was able to show that the teaching of norms for equal participation prevented the high status students in these groups (those who were seen to be better at reading) from dominating the interaction. Morris compared the interaction of treated groups to that of untreated groups who had worked on the survival problem but had received no practice or instruction on group process or on the norm for equal participation. When the interaction of treated and untreated groups playing the game of Shoot the Moon was compared, the difference in rate of participation between the high and low status students in the treated groups was greatly reduced in comparison to the difference in the untreated groups.

The new norms influenced behavior on the new task of Shoot the Moon, even though it was unrelated to the survival problems and nothing was said about using these new behaviors. Students simply assumed that this was the best way to behave in a cooperative task. In other words, the norms had begun to influence group behavior on a new groupwork task without the adult in charge having to say anything!

### The prevention of dominance

Morris taught the students that, if they wanted to survive in a life-threatening situation, they ought to let everyone participate and they ought to listen carefully to each other. It had the effect of quieting down group members who tended to do too much talking and not enough listening. How did this treatment actually work?

Sociologically, the training introduced a new norm for equal participation along with some group process skills. Recall that his groups were initially unequal in reading status, so that we may assume that better readers thought they were going to be more competent on the survival problem. The treatment did *nothing* to interfere with the operation of these expectations for competence.

If that is the case, then why were high status students less active in the treated groups than in the untreated groups? Even though the better readers may have thought they were more competent at the survival problem, the treatment told them that they would hurt the group effort unless they let everyone talk. Thus the new norm interfered with the process just at that point when different expectations turn into different rates of talking in the group.

The data fitted well with this theoretical explanation of what happened. When the treated students were asked about who had the best ideas in the group, they tended to pick the better readers. Thus we see that although the inequality in talking was reduced in the treatment group, status problems were only partially treated.

Although this treatment only partially modifies status problems, it is a safe, simple, and pedagogically sound way to quiet down the members of your class who tend to dominate small groups. Appoint an observer in the group to monitor the use of the desired behaviors. Following the report from the observers, hold a class discussion using the questions listed above. In a classroom situation, it would be good to separate the two survival problems into two practice sessions taking place on different days. Then when you are ready to assign a groupwork task requiring creative problem solving, remind the class of the four features of group process that Morris stressed. They can be displayed permanently in the classroom on a poster.

## Teaching the Norm of Cooperation

In addition to the group process skills and the norm for equal participation, you may wish to include in your training program the idea that cooperative ways of doing things are more *effective* than individuals working alone or individuals competing with one another. This can be especially important for American students of middle-class family backgrounds who have grown up in small families where they have not had to share and work together at home. Many young people and adults in our society are convinced that individual and competitive modes are always more effective than cooperative modes.

The survival problems created by Hall (1971) have the express purpose of demonstrating that a group effort in creative problem solving will lead to better answers than individual efforts. Lost on the Moon is the best known of these tasks and is in wide use in schools. In his study Hall had members of a group individually rank order the items before discussing the problem as a group. He then scored the individual and the group answers according to the ranking developed by survival specialists. It is almost always the case that the group answer is superior to the individual answers on this task. This is a good

way to teach the effectiveness of cooperation in creative problem solving to students in the fifth grade and above.

The successful experience of working together in training
activities will give the students a changed attitude toward cooperative settings. Breer and Locke (1965) studied young
adults in a laboratory setting. In their experiments, people who
had experienced cooperative tasks were more likely to express
a wide range of cooperative values on an attitude and value
questionnaire given some time after the experiment.

As part of your training program you may wish to give
special emphasis to the importance of cooperation as a way of
solving important problems. It can be a central theme in the
study of societies where people work together to insure the
survival of the group.

Bloom and Schunke (1979), working with seventh graders, devised a curriculum to teach students that cooperation is
an efficient and beneficial way to achieve many desirable group
goals. Regular classroom teachers carried out this curriculum
in some of their social studies classes while continuing their
normal activities in others. The Bloom and Schunke curriculum used five tasks. Two of these have already been described
(Lost on the Moon and Jigsaw Puzzles), and the third, Broken Squares, is the original upon which Broken Circles was
based. The fourth task was the preparation of a pantomime.
Each group had to choose an action that could be presented in
a sequence of cues or scenes. The members of the group had
to present these separate actions one by one for the class to
guess the activity. Groups had to decide on the sequence and
to rehearse it. The fifth task was a simulated survival experience to teach students that human beings sometimes have to
work together or they will all die.

Students gained experience in working together toward a
group goal. What distinguishes this curriculum from the training experiences I have already described is that here the
teacher specifically discussed the effectiveness of cooperation
as a method and the problems with noncooperation after each
experience.

In order to measure the effectiveness of this curriculum,
one week after it ended, groups of students were called out of

their classrooms to help develop a simulation activity. In an initial discussion, each group selected a set of rules they preferred to play with. Some options were cooperative and some were competitive. Groups from classes that had used the curriculum were significantly more likely to select the rules that involved working together.

This is a significant study for classroom teachers. It shows how deliberate teaching about cooperation through a series of cooperative tasks will create in students a preference for working in that way, even in a situation outside the classroom.

Bloom and Schuncke did not include any training in group process skills in their program. The behavior of each group was observed and scored for cohesiveness, a "we" feeling. Surprisingly, the untreated groups received a higher score on this measure than the treated groups. The failure of students who had received this experience to exhibit group cohesiveness strongly suggests that the experience of working together is not enough by itself to eliminate problems of interpersonal conflict; desirable new behaviors must be taught.

An intellectual and experiential understanding of the importance of cooperation is a valuable lesson for social studies and particularly for citizenship training. Because this is not enough to provide the skills for working together, you need a training program that combines the teaching of skills for group process *with* learning specifically about the benefits of cooperation from the experience of working together on cooperative tasks.

## COOPERATION AND PROSOCIAL BEHAVIOR

The classroom experimentation of three Israeli researchers (Hertz-Lazarowitz, Sharan, & Steinberg, 1980) shows what can happen when students are exposed for a long time to cooperative groupwork and to specific training for group process. A group of teachers in Israel (Grades 3–7) participated in in-service training to use groupwork involving cooperative planning, group discussions, and cooperative group projects on academic subject matter. Children in their cooperative class-rooms ($N = 243$) were compared to children who had conventional classroom experiences ($N = 150$). In order to evaluate the effects of their classroom experiences, the children were given a series of hypothetical decisions to make. They were asked to divide some chocolates between themselves and their class-mates. If the children were willing to get fewer chocolates for themselves in order to give more to the group, they were scored as more altruistic. If the children chose more chocolates for themselves at the expense of the group, they were scored as more competitive. Finally, if the children were willing to accept fewer if everyone in the group got fewer chocolates, they were scored as more vengeful. Results showed that pupils from cooperative classrooms were much more likely to receive high scores on altruism and lower scores on competition and vengefulness than the pupils from the conventional classrooms.

In a second experiment, groups with five children each from cooperative classrooms were compared to groups from conventional classrooms. Children were asked to recombine letters from an epigram into new words. Groups from treated classrooms were more likely to share answers, to offer help, and to request assistance, whereas the untreated students were more likely to hide their papers from one another, to reject assistance, or to refuse to give assistance. Thus the effects of long-term cooperation in the classroom transfer to new and different situations; children show values and behaviors that we can call prosocial.

## NORMS AS A PRACTICAL CLASSROOM TOOL

Once your training program is completed, the students will be ready for the regular use of groupwork. The fact that new norms have been internalized is of considerable practical importance. Much of the work that teachers usually do will be taken care of by the students for themselves: The group makes sure that everyone understands what to do; the group helps to

keep everyone on task; and group members assist one another. Instead of the teacher having to control everyone's behavior, the students control themselves and others.

Many educators think of training for cooperation as a kind
of moral socialization; they wonder whether this is the function of schools when there are so many other objectives to be
realized through public education. I have presented evidence
in this chapter to show that cooperative training will have these
socializing effects. However, there are entirely different
grounds for arguing that cooperative training is worth the time
it takes from ordinary instruction. Cooperative training allows
the teacher to gain the benefits of group instruction—benefits
in terms of active learning and improved achievement outcomes. If the training results in internalized norms, it has the
added benefit of transferring to any groupwork situation where
the students are reminded that the norms are relevant and
useful. Most important, it frees the teacher from the necessity
of constant supervision and allows the use of professional skills
at a much higher level.

# 5 Planning Groupwork in Stages

Your planning process starts with a basic decision about how students will work together. Deciding how closely students should work together is fundamental to the whole planning process; pros and cons on this issue are discussed below. It is this initial decision that determines the nature of the training program for cooperative skills. The second stage of your planning is deciding on the training program for cooperative skills, described in Chapter 4. We have presented cooperative training first only because it is the first experience of groupwork for the students.

In the third stage of planning, you must create or find the actual tasks your groups will perform. In the fourth stage, you must lay the groundwork with great care. How are the groups to be composed? What instructions and materials must you prepare in advance? How will you physically arrange the classroom? How and when will you assign students to groups? In the fifth and final stage of planning, you will decide how you will evaluate student performance.

Most of your work is completed before the students start their assignments. If your design is a successful one, you have a ready-made formula for success with next year's class as well as a basic format that can be repeated with different tasks for this year's class. By developing one of these designs a year, you can, before long, assemble a fine array of successful curriculum experiences as part of your repertoire.

## PATTERNS FOR WORKING TOGETHER

Will your students work at learning centers, in small short-term discussion groups, in creative problem-solving groups, or in relatively long-term project groups? Or will groupwork consist mostly of peers giving each other assistance on their individual tasks? This is a basic decision that has to be made before anything else can happen. Your choice hangs on two factors: your teaching goals; and how much time and effort you are willing and able to invest in teaching students how to work together.

## Pure Cooperation

Different kinds of groupwork imply different patterns of working together. In order to make a choice, it is useful to compare different groupwork patterns on how closely each requires students to work together. Suppose that you want the students to discuss the meaning of a poem and to arrive at an interpretation that they can present to the rest of the class. You give everyone a copy of the poem and ask that they come to consensus on the final interpretation. This is an example of *pure cooperation*. They must discuss as a group and somehow reject, accept, and synthesize ideas in such a way that everyone will agree.

Other examples of pure cooperation are presenting a group with a word problem in mathematics and asking for a single solution; asking a group to create a mural; requiring a group to develop a solution to a civic, social, or political problem or a moral dilemma. In groupwork that involves pure cooperation, students have to agree on how to solve the problem, make a collective decision, or create a single group product. The group has a single goal or product and has to reach agreement as to how to reach that goal or create that product. This pattern is often called pure cooperation because it requires people to harmonize, compromise, and work closely together throughout every phase of the task.

There is one major problem with pure cooperation. It is costly in terms of interpersonal relations. Some of this cost is reduced by training people for group process skills and by taking time out of assigned tasks for group self-evaluation and interpersonal problem solving. Nevertheless, the group is forced to make negative evaluations of some members' ideas in order to come to agreement. People have to give up some of their favorite ideas in order to compromise with the group. If someone is less than tactful, feelings are hurt and the group must deal with conflict and emotion in order to reach consensus. If the group feels that one member has little to contribute, that person may be ignored and may do nothing but assent to the group decision by a nod.

Perhaps dealing with these problems of human relations is precisely what you are trying to teach. Or perhaps your goal in groupwork is to help students of different races, cultures, or genders to come together to learn how to see each other as people rather than as members of groups or members of the opposite sex. Then by all means, use pure cooperation.

Unless you have such a specific reason for choosing the pure cooperation model, I would strongly recommend alternative methods of working together or a combination of pure cooperation with these other methods. It is easy to modify the pure cooperation model; perhaps the simplest modification is the appointment of one member of each group as a facilitator. This person can be given the special role of seeing to it that the job gets done, that everyone participates, and that the group does not ride roughshod over the feelings of individual members. This simple device greatly eases the pains of pure cooperation. Alternatively, you can use pure cooperation as a single phase of a task, combining it with other phases where different members of the group have different roles to play. Or you can use the simple technique of voting, which has the virtue of making disagreement on the final decision permissible. This is obviously appropriate when you are trying to teach skills for democratic action; you can defuse the tension over reaching consensus with the possibility of a final vote and a minority report.

If your goal is conceptual learning, it is possible to obtain the benefits of interaction without the high costs of pure cooperation. There are two major ways to do this. The first is what I will call the collegial model. In the collegial model, people act as resources and sources of stimulation for each other, assisting each other in many ways, but the products are individual.

The second solution to the problem of pure cooperation is to divide the labor. Members of the group can carry out different portions of the task, or members of the group may be given different roles to play. Although dividing the labor is an effective way to carry out group tasks, it is rarely used in classrooms. (I will devote the next chapter to this practical and powerful way of structuring group tasks.)

## Collegial Model

The use of learning centers described in the last chapter is a good example of the collegial model. Students can be trained to assist each other in solving problems at the learning centers, but individuals can still be responsible for completing some final paper or product. In the simplest version of the collegial model, each group works on the same task. Members are instructed to assist each other in writing, in comprehension of some reading, in solving problems, in the creation of an individual product, or in preparing for a test.

In understanding abstract tasks, retaining the individual product is advantageous; it is important for learners to capture those abstract concepts for themselves. Imagine yourself in a group assigned to solve a complex problem in math. You might understand how members of your group solved the problem after having listened to the discussion, but you might not really grasp the ideas in a way that would transfer to other problems, unless you worked out the problem on paper for yourself.

Students can and do teach each other in the collegial model. This is undoubtedly its major advantage over the conventional method of requiring individuals to work alone. Peer explanations are often excellent, and those who explain often show intellectual gains as a consequence. Furthermore, because students assist each other in understanding your instructions for the task, the number of students who come directly to you for help is reduced. Beyond these ways of helping, students provide inspiration and support for each other. They provide evaluation of the learner's first attempts and can often prevent students from getting stuck, becoming discouraged, or getting off on the wrong track on the assignment. Of course, these advantages do not occur without the preparation for helping others outlined in the previous chapter.

Won't the students copy each other's work? Yes, if they are totally confused by your task instructions. Otherwise, given that you have provided an interesting and challenging task, students will be highly motivated to express themselves and to demonstrate their understanding of the problem. Don't underestimate the motivation of students to demonstrate to themselves as well as to you their increasing level of competence and mastery. Colleagues can help students who are ordinarily convinced that their best efforts will only lead to failure; they give them needed assistance so that these students can tackle the same problems as their classmates who are functioning at grade level.

## CREATING THE TASK

Clearly your choice of task depends on what you want the students to learn. If you are teaching social studies and want the students to experience democracy in action, then you need tasks that require the group to arrive at a collective decision after proper deliberation. If, in contrast, you are trying to increase oral proficiency in English of young children, then you need to find an activity that is so intrinsically interesting that the children will want to talk about it. If you are trying to teach students the elements of paragraph writing, then you may wish to assign the group a task involving the editing of a poorly written composition.

If your goal is more social, such as the reduction of sex stereotyping in the classroom, then you will want to select an engaging task such as making a movie that will allow the group to experience a highly rewarding task through cooperation.

Even though the tasks vary greatly depending on your subject matter and goal, there are some general guidelines for tasks suitable for groups as compared to tasks for individuals. For groupwork choose a task that

- Has more than one answer or more than one way to solve the problem
- Is intrinsically interesting and rewarding
- Allows different students to make different contributions

- Uses multimedia
- Involves sight, sound, and touch
- Requires a variety of skills and behaviors
- Also requires reading and writing
- Is challenging

A task does not work well for groupwork if it

- Has a single right answer
- Can be done more quickly and efficiently by one person than by a group
- Is too low level
- Involves simple memorization or routine learning

## PREPARING THE SITUATION

Give careful thought to instructions for the assignment. They must be sufficiently full and clear so that the group will not become so frustrated and confused that the whole experience will be a sour one for them. Besides, unless you have thought everything through in advance, you will rapidly find yourself trying to be six places at once, straightening out the problems your lack of planning has caused.

Start with a *general orientation session*, stressing the main features of the task and the behaviors that will be required. Don't go on talking too long—students stop listening carefully after a relatively few minutes. If there are difficult new concepts involved, you may want a warm-up lesson where concepts are demonstrated or where students have some chance to acquaint themselves with the major ideas in advance. Equally important in the orientation is reference to cooperative behaviors that will be necessary and any special roles that students will be playing in their groups.

### Written Instructions

Much of the burden of explaining what students are supposed to do can be placed on written instructions for all but the youngest children. (I have seen written instructions work exceedingly well for second graders.) Being able to refer to written instructions, after hearing the main ideas in your orientation, allows the group to figure out what to do for themselves.

Students must be strenuously encouraged to read the instructions and must not be allowed to plunge into the task without knowing what they are doing. This is especially true when there are fascinating materials to observe and manipulate. Even though students who are better readers can simply read the instructions for the others, there is much to be gained in increasing skill in reading comprehension from encouraging everyone to discuss what the instructions say prior to working with materials.

Written instructions must be clear and sufficiently detailed for the group to know what to do without outside assistance. Having tussled with instructions for appliances and do-it-yourself projects, all of us know that writing good instructions is not easy. Some of the problems can be left to the group to solve. By refusing to give a quick answer to requests for help from the group and by encouraging them to solve some of the problems, you can help students learn that they have the capacity to deal with uncertainty for themselves. Other kinds of uncertainty, however, are not functional for the learners. For example, suppose that you have not made clear that you expect the group to prepare a presentation for the class that is based on their collective effort. This lack of clarity in your instructions will lead to a serious misfiring of your plans; correct it for the class as soon as the problem is brought to your attention. You can avoid many of these errors by pretesting your instructions on a fellow teacher, an aide, or a parent volunteer.

The key to writing good instructions is to imagine yourself as a member of the group going through each phase of the task. What information would you need so that you would know what to do next? If, for example, your task implies the use of reference materials or the use of resources outside the classroom, how should that part of the task be done? Should the group make a collective decision on who should go and do that part of the job? When is the group ready to carry out that part of the assignment? Have you suggested any mechanism for coordinating and synthesizing what has been gathered from these outside resources? What considerations should the group keep in mind when preparing for a final class presentation? What is the time allotted, number of members participating, and permissible or suggested forms for presentation?

Although detail is important, instructions should be as simple as possible. Needless confusion comes from adding too many words and alternative ways of explaining things. If you want the group to use some trial and error and to develop some solutions for themselves, tell them to develop their own ways of solving selected problems. Even the youngest groups are quite capable of rising to that challenge.

## Size of Groups

Groups larger than five present problems for participation in interaction. For group discussions, I have always found that four or five is an optimal size. As the group gets larger there is more of a chance that one person will be left out of the interaction almost entirely.

The major argument in favor of groups larger than five is the need for more people for a long-term project where subtasks will be involved. In this case you can plan to let the larger group divide up into task forces to accomplish subgoals. When task forces or subcommittees are used, the size of the group that must discuss and reach consensus should not be greater than five. Alternatively, large groups can divide up the labor so that different people are playing different roles. This will insure that each person makes some contribution to the group.

A group of three has some special problems. There is a strong tendency for two persons to form a coalition, leaving the third feeling isolated and left out. For certain tasks, a pair of students is an ideal group size; for example, if the task is to drill each other on flash cards with spelling words. If the task requires extensive coordination because the persons involved are going to have to arrange to do a series of tasks outside of class hours, keep the group small. Remember that as the group gets larger, arranging times and places for group meetings and activities becomes more and more difficult.

If the group is to manipulate materials, the amount of available workspace is an important consideration. Be sure that the size of the group matches the amount of materials and space available. It is obviously a very poor idea to make some students wait around for materials and a place to work.

## Composing Groups

Groups should be mixed as to academic achievement, sex, and any other status characteristic such as race or ethnicity. This heterogeneity can be achieved by composing groups and assigning students or by allowing students to choose groups according to their interests in special topics that the groups will be studying.

Allowing friends to choose each other for work partners is not a good idea. Students should think of groupwork in terms of work rather than play, and there is clearly a tendency for friends to play, rather than work, when assigned to the same group. Furthermore, some students who are social isolates will not be selected or will actively be rejected for group membership. Teachers sometimes feel that secondary school students will be rebellious if they are forced to work in groups that are not of their own choosing. This will not happen if you orient the class to the purpose of the groupwork and if you are firm and efficient in your assignments.

How can a good mix be created in a class, particularly when you plan to change group assignments as the weeks progress? Here is one simple way to think about the problem of group composition. Considering the nature of the task you have chosen, select certain students who are likely to be a strong resource for any group in which you place them. A resource student may be one who has directly relevant academic skills for the task, who may be a good reader, who has personal experience with the task or with some feature of the task, or who is a creative, articulate, and flexible thinker who responds well to an uncertain and challenging situation. Students who function as resources are not necessarily the more successful students on conventional academic criteria. Another kind of human resource for groupwork is social skill; some students have good social skills that enable them to work very well with others. Such students are of particular benefit to the group; they can help the group deliver whatever it is that they know even if they are not masters of all the required skills.

At the other extreme are students who are, for one reason or another, problematic in your mind. A student who is far behind grade level in basic skills required for the task is one example. Students who have great difficulty in working with others should also be placed in groups with special care. These are often students who will attack and pester their fellow students to get attention, even if that attention is negative. At the younger ages, hyperactive children often represent a great problem to classmates as well as to the teacher.

There should be at least one resource person in each group. Furthermore, problematic individuals should not be concentrated in one group. You should put them with a resource person who can be helpful for their particular problem. Particularly difficult hyperactive children should be put in a group with a resource person who can handle them. Your concern is not only that they should not disrupt and distract the group; you also want to insure that there is someone available in the group who can work with them interpersonally. For students who are problematic because they lack linguistic or academic skills, you need to be sure that there is at least one person in the group who can help them out. This may be a bilingual student who can interpret; or it can be a student who is functioning at grade level. It does not have to be the best student in the class.

As the task changes, different students may join the category of resource persons because of their specialized expertise. As the students gain practice in reading and writing in the group setting, you will note that some problematic students develop to the point where you need no longer worry about them particularly. Further, many more students should be joining the category of resource persons as they gain skills for operating in the groupwork setting. If your groupwork is successful, the majority of the students should be moving into your resource category; there should be very few problematic students. These labels should never be seen as permanent or as indicative of unchanging characteristics of the person. Avoid seeing the resource person as a natural leader; with the development of reading and groupwork skills, most students should be able to function as important resources for others.

In order to make up group assignments, put the name of each student on an index card. Decide how many groups you will have and how big your groups should be. For a given task, select out those who are resources and put at least one in each group. Then select the problematic students and pair them up with a suitable resource. The other students can be sorted into groups, making sure that the end result is a mix with respect to sex, language, and academic ability. To recompose groups for the next task or set of tasks, consider which new students can be called resources and allocate them into groups. Then place problematic students so they are not always paired with the same resource student. The remaining cards can be shuffled like a deck of playing cards. This should result in a good mix, though you should check the resulting assortment within each group.

Waste no time in letting students know their group assignment. Put assignments up on the board along with a map of where groups are to work. Or write the group assignment on top of the task instructions given to each student. If you plan to shift group composition repeatedly over the year, you can make up a series of paper pockets on a chart. Put student names on cards or on tongue depressors. Sort the cards or sticks into pockets, and direct the students to check for their group assignments when they first enter the classroom. Figure 5.1 presents a sample chart.

## Classroom Ecology for Groups

Groups will need space and sufficient freedom from the noise of other people to hear themselves talk. Discussion groups have far less rigorous space demands than groups that are working with materials. They need to be seated so that everyone can see and hear everyone else, preferably in a circle. Irregular seating arrangements will result in very little interaction between those who have to twist around to see each

FIGURE 5.1: Chart Showing Group and Role Assignments

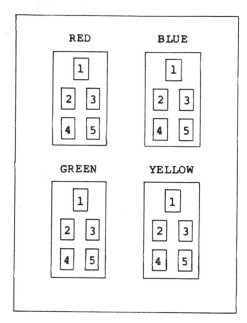

KEY

1. Facilitator
2. Checker
3. Set-up
4. Clean-up
5. Reporter

other. Station the groups as far apart as the room will permit so that they will not be disturbed by each other's discussion. Leave room for yourself to circulate freely between groups.

If you expect group members to work with manipulative materials or with books and written materials, you must plan space for work carefully. Group members should not be kept waiting because they have no space to work. Lack of work space can result in disengagement and general failure of the project. If members do not have adequate room to lay out their task, they may find themselves quite unable to solve the problems; materials tumble off the table, students jostle each other for space, and constructions don't fit together.

Work stations require rearrangement of the tables and chairs from their usual formation. Take into account the question of traffic flow as well as the amount of workspace required. If tables are placed so that they block the free flow of traffic, students will constantly be disturbing one another. It is a good idea to map out your classroom arrangement and consider carefully how people will move about. (If your classroom furniture is inflexible and unsuitable, perhaps you can borrow the multipurpose room or the media center for groupwork.)

Noise is often a special problem for open space schools. If students are working at learning centers, a fair amount of noise is to be expected and is a sign of functioning groups. It is advisable to consult with other teachers who share an open space pod with you well in advance of scheduling groupwork. It should be scheduled simultaneously with their noisier activities.

Every student needs clear access to your instructions. If there is a task card, it should be printed up in fairly large letters and placed where everyone can see it. As an alternative, everyone may have an individual copy of the instructions. The advantage of a common task card is that it brings the groups together immediately in sharing the task of understanding the instructions.

All materials and tools should be pretested to make sure they do what they are supposed to do. Avoid scissors that don't cut and magnets that don't magnetize. Although it may seem sensible to keep things like scissors and glue at a central location, it is actually more efficient to set these out at each learning station where they will be needed. With decentralized materials, there is far less rushing to and fro with its distracting consequences.

Teachers of elementary students must be concerned with the safety of sharp tools and with the use of heat and fire. The usual solution is to attempt to station an adult to supervise these activities directly. This is actually a costly solution in terms of using up scarce adult resources. One good alternative solution is to include a discussion of strategies for dealing with potentially dangerous materials in your orientation. Another solution is to appoint one of the children as a safety officer, with a clear understanding of what he or she should watch for and under what circumstances an adult should be called in.

Setting up work stations with instructions and materials sounds like too much work for the average busy teacher. It is! The students should be trained to do the work of setting up these stations; they should move the furniture and set out the materials needed. If the teacher lists or pictures what will be needed on the task card, the student in charge of setting up can get the materials from cupboards or storage areas, provided that these places are properly labeled (with pictures for non-readers). And there is certainly no excuse for teachers having to clean up after the work is done; students will cheerfully carry out these tasks if it is made clear that this is part of their job. First graders can do an excellent job of cleaning and setting up; they appear to relish the responsibility.

Solving challenging intellectual problems in a group will stimulate the students to seek out more information. They will often need resources such as reference books and dictionaries as part of their task. If everyone will need certain reference works like the dictionary, put them on something with wheels so groups can easily bring the heavy volumes around to the work station.

Students will want to read and learn more about the subject of their group task. Especially with students who need to be encouraged to learn to dig for information and to read books on subjects that have aroused their interest, make these informational resources easily accessible. Place relevant books from the library right near the learning center where the students are working on a particular topic. Display pictures, maps, posters, and objects near the work stations that will stimulate the students to ask questions, think more, and dig further into the subject. A great advantage of this strategy is that if one group has finished its work before the other groups, the materials for obvious extension of the activity are all prepared. The teacher can with a few minutes of discussion and questioning help the group to push the investigation further with the materials at hand.

## PLANNING EVALUATION

How can you evaluate student performance when the task is done by a group? When I present a session on groupwork techniques, teachers invariably ask this question. The first step is to disentangle the issue of learning from the issue of giving grades and marks. For most teachers, the need for students to get feedback on their work is fused with the responsibility to give students grades.

Start with the assumption that groups and individuals need to have some way of finding out if they are "on the right track" in solving problems. They need to know how what they have done measures up to some set of intellectual criteria and what they can do to improve their product. This is the issue for learning and needs to be considered quite apart from grading. There are many ways to provide feedback for learning.

Some groupwork tasks have the happy quality of built-in evaluation. Consider a task like making a device operate or an electric bulb light up. The students can tell for themselves whether or not they are successful. If they are unsuccessful and are consequently frustrated, you can help them, *not by showing them how to do it properly*, but by encouraging them to try some new strategies, to go back to the instruction card, or to try out the ideas of all the members of the group. Don't be afraid to let the students struggle; that is the only way they will really come to grasp more abstract concepts—people learn from mistakes.

It is not always necessary to evaluate whether students have gotten the ideas after each groupwork task. Very often, in selecting a series of groupwork tasks, the best strategy is to provide a number of varied opportunities to grasp the same abstract ideas. To expect that all students will grasp an abstract idea like bar graphing from a single groupwork task is totally unrealistic. Students will need to have repeated experiences with the concept before they grasp it in such a way that they will be able to recognize and deal with the concept in new settings. Some students may utterly fail to get the idea in one task but may suddenly begin to understand in another setting. If you become overly concerned too early in the process with whether each student is mastering the content of each groupwork assignment, you will find yourself insisting that students get the right answer to every task, thus short-circuiting their whole process of inquiry.

If you want to know whether or not students are making some progress, design an individual worksheet for each group task. Let the students use each other as resources in solving the problem, but ask each student to finish an individual product. Not only does this method help students firm up what they have learned, but it provides you with a way to check up on their progress. If you have avoided overly simple "right answer" tasks for the groupwork assignment, then different students can learn different things from the same task. If the tasks have this open character, then you will not necessarily use standardized criteria to provide feedback to individual students. You can provide some individual feedback to students by asking key questions and by pointing out what they have grasped and what they need to work on. You can even ask the students to do the activity again or to rewrite the worksheet.

The custom of pulling students back together as a whole group for a wrap-up at the end of each groupwork session is an excellent way of providing feedback. You can pick out a student who has obviously grasped the central idea or has a product illustrating an important concept and have that student explain what he has learned. This has the double function of reinforcing this learner and assisting the rest of the class in preparation for that activity. Hold a discussion during a wrap-up in which group members discuss how well they have done on using cooperative behaviors featured in the training program. Remember that the class needs feedback on their group process as well as on their products.

How can a group product be evaluated? You can provide feedback to the group, remembering that it should always be honest, clear, and specific about what the group did well and where it could improve. General comments such as "Great job!" may make the group feel good, but they will do very little to promote learning.

## Peer Evaluation

During any process of group interaction, there will be a constant process of peer evaluation. This is an unavoidable part of group interaction. One of the advantages of groupwork is that many students can help extend your power to teach by providing feedback to peers. Of course, you may want to include some work on giving constructive feedback as part of your training program. Peers can be merciless with each other.

If the criteria for evaluation are clear, students can learn to evaluate each other's group product. If each group displays its work in some way, students can be taught what criteria are legitimate and how to give constructive criticism. This strategy enables the group to obtain feedback at the same time that it teaches a valuable intellectual and social lesson to the class.

If you feel that the groups need some improvement in their group processes, ask each group to stop their activities and spend five minutes discussing how well they are doing according to the behaviors included in the cooperative training program (which should be on permanent display in the classroom). Self-criticism is a powerful way to reinforce the training program. Peers will act to bring each other into conformity with the desired ways of behaving.

## Testing and Grading

Many proponents of cooperative groupwork recommend giving a group grade for a group project. This has the effect of making individuals dependent on the group effort for a satisfactory evaluation. It has the drawback of making the peer evaluation process that takes place within the group rather harsh. If one group member is felt to be incompetent at the task, the group is likely to forbid him or her to have any part in the product. The student who is perceived to have the most relevant knowledge will be encouraged to take over the task on his or her own. It is therefore preferable to provide feedback on group products instead of grading them.

Many teachers feel that unless the group product is graded, students will not be motivated. If the task is challenging and interesting, and if students are sufficiently prepared for skills in group process, students will experience the process of groupwork itself as highly rewarding. Knowing that they will receive some feedback on their product will also help motivate them to complete the task.

Should groups compete with each other for grades or prizes on their group product? Competition has the effect of increasing motivation of students; for that reason many teachers cannot envision groupwork without some such external set of rewards. Such competition has at least two drawbacks: It will aggravate the problem of status within the group because low status students will be seen as harmful to the group's chances of winning, and it will encourage the students to believe that learning is not intrinsically rewarding but that one ought to be paid for such drudgery by something external to the learning task itself. If the tasks are rich, as has been suggested, there will be no need for such crutches to provide motivation.

Following any series of groupwork tasks designed to teach certain skills or concepts, you can of course design an examination to test the individuals' grasp of those concepts. This will provide the formal occasion for grading. Help the students to use groups in preparing for the exam. Students who have worked through the tasks will be well prepared to help each other in studying for the exam. If students have produced compositions, using each other as resources, these individual products could be graded.

If the tasks consist of materials that must be mastered by rote learning, then competition between groups can be of value in motivating students. The use of competitive team learning has been shown to be very effective in producing learning gains for less successful students (Slavin, 1983). Slavin advocates a team score based on how well members of the team do on an examination. Team members help to prepare each other for the exam. The scores of students are based on the amount of improvement individuals show in comparison to the last testing; the team is not penalized for members whose entering achievement level is low. On the contrary, these may be the team members who will show the most dramatic individual learning gains, not only because they have received help on reading comprehension, but also because group pressure keeps them thoroughly engaged with the task.

Never grade or evaluate students on their individual contributions to the group product. Even if it were true that a student contributed almost nothing, it is never clear that the student is at fault. Other students may have acted to exclude him or her from the process. Something about the task instructions or the group process may be at fault. It is better to look on such an event as a failure of the groupwork technique rather than a failure of the individual student. Moreover, telling students that their individual contributions will be evaluated will have the effect of making lower status students unwilling to risk active participation. In a study of junior high school groups, Awang Had (1972) found that younger students were much less willing to speak up and participate in groups where they were told that their individual contributions would be evaluated than in groups where they were told that the group product would be evaluated.

In review, by separating the necessity for feedback in the learning process from the grading issue, the problem of what to do becomes much less difficult. Feedback can often be accomplished by peers as well as by teachers. It can take place while the groups are at work, in individual conferences with the teacher, or during a wrap-up. Including a wrap-up each day at the close of a groupwork session is invaluable for feedback on both process and product.

Teachers can meet their responsibilities for giving grades by designing some individual products of groupwork and by testing students for their grasp of the basic concepts the group tasks were designed to teach. Properly designed groupwork can produce major gains, even on standardized achievement tests.

## A WORD ABOUT TIME

After making detailed plans, it is necessary to estimate how much time each phase will take. How much time will be needed for pretraining? Will the students have time for their first groupwork experience after the orientation? If the orientation goes on too long, the students will be frustrated by having to end the groupwork too early, or there will be no time for a wrap-up. Making a realistic time schedule for each phase (and sticking to it) is an indispensable management tool.

# 6 Giving Everyone a Part to Play

Here are two illustrations from the work of two teams of beginning high school teachers. In each case, one of the pair worked as the teacher and the other functioned as observer. The first case took place in the high school social studies class of David Payne, an intern teacher. Here is the observer's report.

Groups of students are playing Monopoly, but this is no ordinary game. One group is starting out with $100 per participant, while another starts out with $400; as the game proceeds, more money is added into the system. When someone lands on a piece of property, everyone except the property holder bids; the property holder gets to keep the proceeds. Mr. Payne explains that these students are studying the effects of increasing money supply on the inflation of property values. He provides us with a copy of the instructions given to the students. Each group has four players, and each person has a special role in addition to that of being a Monopoly player:

a) Banker: Dispenses money to each player; using calculator, keeps track of amount of money in system.

b) Grapher: Plots on the graph the total money in the system in relation to the purchase price of the lots.

c) Facilitator: Keeps the game flowing smoothly; presides over bidding and makes sure all make four trips around the board within the hour.

d) Synthesizer: Presents the group's finding concerning the relation of money supply to prices.

Two other students in the class observe the games in progress. Their job is to graph the average money in circulation against the average cost of property of the groups. This pair is expected to show how the supply of money has affected the prices of property.

The students appear intrigued and engaged in the competition. The girls are at first more reticent about bidding aggressively, but they become much more active as they become comfortable with the rules and strategy. All the students are managing their special roles. One student is having a little trouble with plotting points; the others help. The teacher seems to be forgotten. In one game a student is trying to dominate the bidding process, but now he has run out of money, so he is suddenly very quiet. Class time passes very rapidly. There is no time for a wrap-up today, but the two students who have plotted the averages are told that they will be expected to make a presentation first thing tomorrow. (Payne & Strutner, 1984, pp. 3–4)

In the second case, the observer is reporting on Mike Leonard's class in Geometry, a Lower-Track Math Class. Mike Leonard is also an intern teacher.

This is a casual and friendly group of students who appear to relate well to each other and to their teacher. Mr. Leonard begins the lecture with a short review of last night's homework. This work covers skills needed in today's groupwork. He uses an overhead projector; the class has many questions. Mr. Leonard then goes over the assignment. Each member has at least one equation of a line for which he or she must find three ordered pairs in the relation, draw the graph of the relations, find the slope of the graph and find the y intercept of the graph. The group has the responsibility of writing an explanation of the $y = ?$ Mr. Leonard has placed graph paper and a straight edge on each desk before class.

He now reads and explains information written on the board. This includes a list of behaviors expected in the role of facilitator: (1) makes sure everyone participates; (2) makes sure task is completed in 20 minutes; (3) gets help from teacher if entire group cannot answer a question.

The groups have been prearranged so that students already know their group and their location. The facilitator's role is a rotating one; and today's facilitators are given tags to indicate their special function. One person has the role of grapher who must graph all equations on one set of axes and label them neatly.

Next, Mr. Leonard asks the students to get into their groups and begin work. It is apparent that he has trained his students well beforehand because it takes less than a minute for all the students to be in groups and involved in the task. Once in their groups, certain students are still unclear as to what the task involves, but other members explain it to them. All the students certainly seem to be engaged in their work. Even those that Mr. Leonard has described as "academically weak" seem involved and active. Some students need help in understanding how to find ordered pairs and in graphing lines; they receive explanations from other members of the group. The facilitators start out by leading, but as time goes by the other students are doing as much directing and "facilitating" as the person assigned to that role.

The students begin by clarifying the task among themselves and by choosing someone to play the role of the grapher; they then move into their separate tasks, working out their lines and points. The graphers are interested in pushing everyone to complete and pass the graphs on to them so that they can finish their job. In the last phase, the collective group discusses an explanation, while the graphers produce their summary graph. The assignment is done in twenty minutes. Mr. Leonard now puts up on the board the graphs from the groups—all are correct. He writes all the equations on the board and proceeds to ask questions. Interestingly, several groups are able to give variations on the correct answers. This takes ten minutes, and there are still five minutes left to hand out a review sheet for the test tomorrow and an evaluation questionnaire on the groupwork. (Kinney & Leonard, 1984, pp. 9–12)

## EFFICIENT AND EFFECTIVE GROUPS

How do these two beginning teachers avoid most of the problems of nonparticipation and interpersonal difficulties in their groups? The secret of their success lies partly in their careful planning and preparation and partly in the way they have given each member something specific to do or a role to play. This is one of the most efficient methods of designing a smooth-functioning and productive group. These methods reduce problems of one or more members' making no contribution to the group or one member's dominating the group. In groups where members have different roles and jobs to do, they feel very satisfied with their part in the group process.

When each group member is doing a part of the job, there is a *division of labor*. Mr. Leonard's assignment is an excellent example: each student has to do one equation, but the results of all equations are necessary to the final product.

When each person's job is given a name and is accompanied by a list of expected behaviors, group members have been assigned specific roles to play. Notice that the two cases display a wide variety of roles: banker, grapher, facilitator, synthesizer. In both these cases, although each person has a separate job to do (the labor is divided to some extent), the group cannot function without the work of all its members. In the case of the Monopoly game, the group will not produce its graph unless everyone plays the game and everyone plays his or her special role. In the math assignment, there are individual tasks in one phase, but there is an initial planning phase and a final discussion phase that require collective action. Thus, close cooperation is often necessary even when everyone has a different part to play.

## LEADERSHIP ROLES

There are advantages to the use of leaders. In the adult world of work, there are very few leaderless groups or examples of pure cooperation. When one person is an appointed leader, there is less jockeying for influence among the members than in leaderless groups because the status order is clear (the leader is in charge); the leader is seen as legitimate, that is, backed up by higher authority. When every decision does not have to be made by consensus, the group's operation is quicker and more efficient.

The teacher has it well within her power to appoint group leaders for each of the collective task groups. Furthermore, the teacher has the authority to say exactly what the group leader has the right and duty to do with respect to the group.

From an educational point of view, the use of a strong leader has some drawbacks. Group members may have very little to do with each other and may simply respond to the leader's directions. If the task involves a group discussion, a strong leader is likely to dominate. Members will tend to listen more to the group leader concerning the content of the task, even though other group members may have more valuable ideas. Furthermore, if the leader is constantly saying whose turn it is to talk, the amount of interchange between group members is greatly reduced. A classroom group leader with the power to direct discussion and to make final decisions will often cause the group to give up and to let the leader do the whole task.

How can the classroom teacher insure the efficiency of a leader without sacrificing the active learning that takes place during creative interchange? One solution is to use leaderless groups only for selected phases. Keep in mind that consensus groups with no formal leadership and no division of labor are very costly in terms of interpersonal relations and the level of social skills required. They are likely to exhibit status problems where one person dominates the group or status struggles in which several persons grapple for dominance. Therefore, only short-term use of such leaderless groups is recommended.

If the project is long-term, one possibility is to pull out those stages or phases of the task in which exchange and creative problem solving are most critical. These particular stages can have a leaderless-group structure, while all the rest of the project can benefit from combinations of division of labor and special roles for different group members, including leadership roles. Recall that creative interchange will not be accomplished without some sort of special training and socialization of norms for behavior during group discussion.

Two of the stages of a long-term project that benefit from creative interchange are the initial planning session and the integration of the final product. Initial planning sessions require open and creative exchange for several reasons. Obviously the project's outcome is largely determined by the depth of the analysis of the problem and the quality of the decisions. If the students are discussing a social studies project on Pueblo dwellings, their final report or presentation is only as good as their analysis of what are the important materials to be gathered and which activities are to be carried out by individual group members. At a more advanced level of scholarship, if the group is asked to do some library research on one aspect of inflation in order to write a group paper, the quality of that paper is partially dependent on the initial intellectual analysis.

In addition to this primarily intellectual reason for desiring a thorough and open discussion of the initial plans for the project, there is an important social-psychological reason for making everyone an equal and full participant in the initial planning phase. Unless members feel that they have a strong stake in the decisions that are made, they are likely to lose motivation when difficulties develop in carrying out their tasks. If, in contrast, all feel that they have had a fair chance to contribute to the initial plans and have accepted the group's decision only after arguing out the issue fully and accepting or compromising in some reasonable fashion, there will be fewer members who let the group down by failing to do their jobs. Other members will feel free to say, "You took part, and you agreed that this was a reasonable way to do the job. So now you have to do your part!"

When the pieces of the final product have been assembled, the group is ready for another phase that requires an open interchange. A leaderless group can be used again at this time. Particularly if the group has been through a period where members have been on their own, researching or creating materials for the final product, the group needs to learn what each member has found out. Although some of this process can take place through reading and examining the reports of individual members, major intellectual benefits come from evaluating, analyzing, and synthesizing what each person has learned. This discussion can cause the group to look at the problem in new and different ways. Integration is a challenging task intellectually as well as interpersonally. Criticism and evaluation from others are never easy to take, but they are essential for a good final product.

During the middle phase when the labor has been divided up, people can go about their business in a fairly independent way. At this stage, it is desirable to have a leader who acts as a center for group communication and who keeps everything moving forward.

## Limited Leadership Techniques

There is a second solution to the dilemma of leaders. If the leadership role is properly structured to foster creative interchange, a group can have the benefits of pure cooperation and the efficiency of a leader for a short- or long-term task. A facilitator, for example, can act as a limited leader.

The limited leader is not a boss with executive decision-making rights. Everyone in the group understands that the facilitator does not control the decisions or the content of the discussion. The functions of the facilitator are limited to seeing to it that everyone participates, keeping the group on task and away from irrelevancies, or making sure that the group makes clear decisions in the time the teacher has allotted.

The use of a facilitator has the advantage of efficiency because one member is in charge of making sure that the job gets done on time. It has the added advantage of preventing status struggles and domination by members of the group who have high academic or social standing. No doubt something in the way of a free and full exchange of the well-trained leaderless group is given up, but like so many decisions in designing groupwork, there is a tradeoff in the relative advantages and disadvantages of each technique.

A facilitator can accomplish many objectives for the teacher. Payne's facilitator was responsible for keeping the Monopoly game flowing and for supervising the bidding, while Leonard used a facilitator to make sure that everyone participated, to get the job done in time, and to represent the group in asking for the teacher's help. These were both limited leadership roles; they were different from each other and tailor-made to the particular tasks.

To summarize, the facilitator helps the group to

- Give everyone a chance to talk
- Give reasons for ideas
- Give different ideas
- Listen to each other's ideas

## Assigning Limited Leadership Roles

How can you make sure that groups will accept the leadership of the facilitator? There are three things you must do to insure the effectiveness of this or any other role you wish to assign:

1. Make your assignment of the job to a specific member of each group public knowledge—everyone must clearly know that you have given this person the authority to act as facilitator.
2. Specify exactly what the facilitator is supposed to do.
3. Make sure that everyone knows what the facilitator is supposed to do.

Try writing out the facilitator's job on a large chart and leave it where everyone can see it. This will help to clarify the role; it will also make everyone understand that the facilitator is only doing what the teacher has directed. When this is done, even the meekest student will be willing to step forward and be a facilitator if you ask, and group members will treat that person with respect. Suppose the facilitator tries to quiet down someone who is doing too much of the talking: "I think the group understands what you've been saying; we need to hear some other ideas." Unless the target of this remark understands that the job of facilitator involves giving everyone a chance to contribute, he or she is likely to view such a remark as a personal insult. The object of all this clarity, specificity, and publicity is to have group members understand that the leader is behaving in a certain way only because he or she is expected to do so as part of the job.

In selecting students for leadership positions, don't try to pick people on the basis of "leadership quality." Give everyone a chance to play the role of facilitator at one time or another. Because teachers often believe that few students have the capacity for leadership, they tend to pick the most successful student or the most popular or athletic student. Natural social leaders are also picked for a very practical reason: Teachers are sometimes afraid that unless they win over such students, they will be the source of trouble during the groupwork.

It is true that under ordinary classroom and playground conditions only a few students are capable of persuading others to do as they say. But the conditions in groupwork are different in important ways. The facilitator does not have to assert leadership in an informal group. Instead, he or she has been *assigned* to play a specific role in a specific group by the teacher. Under these conditions a student with ordinarily low or middling status in the classroom will have little difficulty in guiding a group. If the role is clearly and publicly defined, and if students are properly prepared for any skills that will be called for (see below), a wide variety of students can be excellent facilitators.

The opportunity to play such a role is a much-needed boost to the status of many students in the classroom who are seen as meek, mild, or incompetent. It is especially important that girls get the chance to play leadership roles; very few girls are spontaneously seen as leaders by teachers or by peers (Lockheed, Harris, & Nemceff, 1983). Lastly, when there are only a few minority students, appointing one of them to be a leader is important in combating the sense of powerlessness they may feel in a classroom with few students like themselves and in a school with few teachers or administrators of their racial or ethnic background.

### Training facilitators

Suppose that you want a facilitator to ensure a rich discussion. Typical fifth graders do not have a clear idea of what a good discussion is, nor do they have many tactful strategies for persuading group members to change their behaviors.

Therefore, unless you are sure they have the skills, it is wise to train the potential facilitators to carry out their jobs.

Wilcox (1972) demonstrated that it is possible to train fifth- and seventh-grade students from inner-city classrooms to be facilitators. Her study compared groups with trained student leaders to groups with untrained student leaders and to groups led by teachers. Her task was the discussion of a moral dilemma; the students were to come to agreement as to what was the best thing to do. Thus her task demanded consensus. Her groups were interracial and mixed in academic achievement. If she had not interfered by using a facilitator, the stage was set for domination by high status members of the student groups.

Students in groups with trained student leaders were significantly more active than students in teacher-led groups or students working with untrained student leaders. Furthermore, the quality of the contributions of the members of groups with trained student leaders was more original and diversified than the quality of student response in groups working with teachers. In the teacher-led discussion groups responses were more conventional, partly because the teachers often felt it necessary to moralize whenever a student response suggested unconventional morality. The results with untrained student leaders were highly variable; some looked as good as groups with trained student leaders while the techniques of others left much to be desired.

Wilcox posted a chart with questions that the groups were to discuss. In addition, she posted explicit criteria for what makes a good group discussion:

- Give everyone a fair turn.
- Give reasons for ideas.
- Give different ideas.

She chose student leaders who were neither the most nor the least socially powerful members of their classrooms.

Those students selected to be trained student leaders were given the job of helping the group meet the three criteria for a good group discussion. During the initial training session group leaders were told the following:

> "Boys and girls, we're going to see slides and hear a story about some children who have a problem—and you've been chosen to lead the discussion after we hear the story. This morning we're going to talk about and practice how to be a leader. There are different ways a person can be a leader. Different people have different ideas about what it means to be a good leader. Some people think being a leader means telling everyone what to do practically all the time. Some people think a good leader means letting everyone do just as he pleases—not interfere with their fun. And some think—and this is my idea too—that a good leader is in between these two. I think being a good leader means being part of a good group—talking with the other members—letting everyone tell his ideas—being just like the other members—so long as everything is going okay.
>
> "But if things are not okay, then the good leader knows how to help his group. When wouldn't things be going okay?" (Children may suggest, and if not, trainer mentions the silent group, the non-participator, the monopolizer.) "If someone in the group never gives anyone else a chance to talk—or if one person doesn't talk—a good leader can help by asking questions—or reminding the big talker that someone else needs a chance. We'll talk about how to do this without making others angry. But remember—the good leader uses these ideas only when they're needed. Most of the time the good leader is just like everyone else in the group, listening and taking turns talking." (Wilcox, 1972, p. 145)

The leaders were then shown a training film of a group discussion with a leader who talked more than necessary. In the discussion that followed concerning the performance of this leader, the trainer noted any comments directed to the three criteria for a good discussion. For each suggestion the trainer actually rehearsed with the leaders how they could get the group to adhere to the criteria. The students then role-played a discussion such as they would lead. They were directed to stop the group discussion after about five minutes and ask members to evaluate how well they were doing by the criteria on the suggestions chart.

This initial training session took thirty minutes. There were shorter follow-up training periods before the second and third sessions of each group to help the leaders with participation problems they experienced.

Note the way Wilcox stressed a limited leadership role, so that the student leaders would not become dominant, particularly while the group was making a final decision. She made sure they would recognize undesirable leader behavior by making a special training film, but there are less elaborate ways to accomplish this objective. One might role-play the leader who dominates the group discussion or ask one of the students to play this role, or one might tape record a simulated session with an overly dominant facilitator. When Wilcox felt that special skills would be necessary to enforce desired behavior, she provided strategies and opportunities for practice for the leaders-in-training. Finally, in the follow-up session, she provided feedback on the problems they were experiencing.

This is not the only way to train facilitators. It does, however, illustrate the importance of clearly defining the role and carefully preparing new skills. Regardless of the age of the students, the instructor should always try to achieve this kind of clarity and should stop to analyze whether or not appointed facilitators have the skills necessary to carry out the role.

### Group harmonizer

The basic idea of the facilitator can be elaborated into two limited leadership roles. One person might be assigned the job of moving the group through its agenda, getting everyone's opinion; another member might be assigned the role of group harmonizer—easing interpersonal conflicts that arise and being attentive to the feelings of individual members. In a training program that divides task and socioemotional functions of leadership roles, Schmuck and Schmuck (1979, p. 86) provide some excellent components of this second role:

1. Encouraging: being friendly, warm, and responsive to others; accepting others and their contributions; listen-

ing, showing regard for others by giving them an opportunity for recognition.
2. Expressing group feelings: sensing feeling, mood, and
relationships within the group; sharing own feelings
with other members.
3. Compromising: offering to compromise own position,
ideas, or status; admitting errors; disciplining oneself
to help maintain the group.

Other roles are those of recorder of the group, representative
of the group to a coordinating committee for the entire class,
and spokesperson or reporter for the group to the class as a
whole.

## Roles for Students of Particular Ages

With more mature groups who have the task of synthesizing individual productions into a written or oral report, an
excellent specialized role is that of summarizer (or synthesizer). The summarizer works with a chalkboard or butcher
paper in front of the group, putting down key ideas under
discussion. The summarizer is not merely recording; he or she
leaves out irrelevant issues and highlights disagreements between ideas that will need to be resolved. The advantage of this
role is that it tends to depersonalize disagreement; the argument is between *ideas* rather than between individuals who
proposed the ideas. The group gains objectivity, and those who
are unwilling to say negative things about each other's ideas
face-to-face are able to be objectively critical when faced with
ideas-separate-from-persons.

Another useful role is that of resource person. This member of the group has the responsibility of making sure the
group uses the materials relevant for discussion. I often plan a
lesson around a minilecture accompanied by a handout concerning the major concepts. In the groupwork task that follows the lecture, the groups are asked a series of questions that
requires them to use and apply the concepts. The resource
person makes sure that the group utilizes the handout, often
searching out answers to questions raised by the group during

the discussion. In this group design I also employ a facilitator, a spokesperson, and a synthesizer.

Young children love to play roles that entail clear responsibilities. When students are young, the teacher must take more time to develop these roles clearly and to ensure that the children have the skills involved. Furthermore, these roles must be discussed and reinforced in the wrap-up following each session.

A good example of a set of roles for young children are those used by teachers of second through fifth grades for *Finding Out/Descubrimiento*, a bilingual program designed by De Avila and Duncan (1980) to develop thinking skills. The system I developed for this approach uses heterogeneous groups of four or five children assigned to each of five or six learning centers. All classrooms use facilitators; teachers select from the other roles on the list below to suit their own students:

*Facilitator:* Sees to it that everyone gets the help he or she needs to do the task; is responsible for seeking answers to questions within the group; teacher is only queried if no one in the group can help.

*Checker:* Makes sure that everyone has finished his or her worksheet, answering all the questions.

*Set-up:* Is responsible for setting up all the materials at the learning center. These are stored in such a way that a child can easily gain access to the materials needed. Pictures help to tell the child which materials will be needed and where they will be placed.

*Clean-up:* Is responsible for putting away materials properly and wiping off table.

*Safety Officer:* Is responsible during tasks involving heat or sharp edges for supervising others and for notifying adult of potentially dangerous situations.

*Reporter:* Is responsible for telling what group found out during wrap-up.

There is a large chart indicating the group, learning center, and role for the day for each child. Second and third graders wear large badges of different colors indicating their

roles. If someone in the group is absent, one child will cheerfully play two roles (and get to wear two buttons or badges).
Roles are rotated over time, giving everyone a chance to play
every role during the year.

## DIFFERENT WAYS TO DIVIDE THE LABOR

There are so many ways to divide up the work within
groups and between groups that the actual limit is set only by
the teacher's imagination. Just to start you imagining the possibilities, let me present three examples.

First, you might stage a debate. Assign each group in the
class a different point of view on a controversial issue. Their
task will be to prepare an argument from that point of view.
The final project is a panel discussion or debate in front of the
class.

A second suggestion is to use the expert technique. Divide
the class into groups with each group asked to prepare the answers to a different set of study questions. Students are told
that they must make sure that each person in the group will be
able to function as an expert on the answers to their set of
questions in the second phase. For the second phase, divide up
the experts so that there is one expert for each set of questions
in each group. Then instruct the group to go over all questions with the resident expert acting as discussion leader for his
or her set of questions. This is an adaptation of Aaronson's
(1978) Jigsaw Method. I would recommend it only for classes
where students are fairly secure in their reading skills. Otherwise, an "expert" may experience public failure because he or
she cannot master the study materials.

As a third suggestion, you can break up the task so that
each person plays a different and complementary role; a technical team such as an airplane crew or an operating room team
operates in this way. People work together very closely, but
each has a different job to do. I have used this method with
great success at an interracial summer school where students
were divided into interracial groups for the purpose of making movies (Cohen, Lockheed, & Lohman, 1976). The roles

were divided into camera person, director, storywriter, actor, and so forth. Over the weeks of the summer school, each student played each role. For the interracial situation this technique has the great advantage of teaching the students that different people can make very different and creative contributions to the group, if given the chance to play a specialized role.

## THE GROUP INVESTIGATIVE METHOD

In the final section of this chapter, I would like to describe in some detail the "Group Investigative Method" developed by Sharan and Hertz-Lazarowitz (1980). This technique uses both division of labor and a variety of leadership roles. Group investigation is recommended for teachers who want to develop higher order cognitive processes such as critical evaluation, adjusting to other people's intellectual perspective, synthesis, and analysis. Another objective is to provide students with the experience of making decisions about future activities and carrying through with their responsibilities in an adult manner.

In order to accomplish these objectives, Sharan and Hertz-Lazarowitz (1980) have recommended groups that continue functioning over time in order to accomplish long-term projects that are presented to the class as a whole. In order to solve the problems of interpersonal process, various leadership roles and some training in group process skills are included. Teachers who use this technique receive extensive in-service training as a team from a selected school.

The group investigative method assumes that knowledge does not develop from a simple input-and-storage process. Rather, it stresses the ability of a group to produce meaning as a result of collective effort. Social interaction and communication play a vital role in the pupils' construction of knowledge.

A class engaged in group investigation has a set of small groups, each numbering from two to approximately six students. The groups engage in a collective effort to study a given topic for a specified period of time. Usually, groups study different aspects of the same general topic. Each group plans specific content and methods of study, carries out its study plan, and prepares and presents it to the entire class in some form. The intellectual skills required for this complex task are those of reading comprehension, summarizing, efficient use of reference books, evaluation, analysis, and integration of one's ideas and information with the work of others.

In the initial stage, there is an elaborate process of identification and selection of group study topics through cooperative planning by all students. Special groups are created just for the purpose of developing lists and ideas of aspects of the topic that might be studied. The teacher plays an active role in helping synthesize these ideas into a final list of topics that will incorporate suggestions from a large number of people. Topics chosen for group investigation should involve a wide range of intellectual skills; they should allow for alternative answers, solutions, and approaches and should permit a variety of final products as an alternative to oral or written reports. The students are allowed to select which topic and group they will work with, so that the initial planning groups and project groups do not have the same membership. This stage allows students to develop an initial commitment to a group out of their own interests and to freely choose their groups.

The groups must then plan the learning task, determining subtopics for each member and how they will work together. The teacher assists groups at this stage in choosing learning tasks that are not limited to gathering information but involve active investigation. For example, a learning task might be to go out and interview some people on a topic rather than to copy out information from the encyclopedia. A variety of sources should be used for the intellectual activities, leading to a variety of ideas, opinions, and evaluation. The group must also look ahead to the kind of group product they want to produce. This forces them to coordinate their tasks to an intellectual goal.

The longest stage is the one in which the investigation is carried out. Although this involves considerable division of labor, there is a continuing need for communication, coordination, and conference between students and between students and teacher. During this stage the teacher may have to stress group skills and individual study skills.

The final stage involves preparing the final product. The products of each group must be integrated so as to make a coherent presentation. Sharan and Hertz-Lazarowitz (1980) recommend a classroom coordinating committee with a representative from each project group. The function of this committee is to keep track of the progress of individual groups and to plan ahead as to how each product will be combined into a coherent series of experiences for the class. The general topic for study might be an investigation of the California missions, life in the original American colonies, the respiratory or circulatory system, or the influence of Japan on the modern American economy. For younger children, simple books, filmstrips, and direct observation can be substituted for more elaborate resource materials.

Several other strategies are recommended for tying together the curriculum unit. Learning centers can be developed where students can be required to study materials that the instructor wants everyone to master as background. Lastly, the class may be asked to study each other's projects carefully in preparation for an examination that is made up of questions submitted by each group on their materials.

Throughout this lengthy process, groups are managed by having different members play chairperson. The chair may be asked to present a topic, to keep track of time, to distribute written material, to summarize previous discussion, to focus discussion on a topic, or to encourage maximum participation. There are also roles such as recorder and representative to the coordinating committee.

In a three-week experiment with 217 pupils from ten classrooms in Grades 2–6, Sharan, Hertz-Lazarowitz, and Ackerman (1980) evaluated the type of learning taking place in five classrooms using this small-group method in contrast to five classrooms using traditional methods to teach the same materials. The evaluation test used items of lower and higher cognitive levels, as defined by Bloom's taxonomy. In three out of five grades, the small-group classrooms did significantly better on higher level questions. The direction was as predicted in the other grades but did not reach statistical significance. On the lower level questions, the two groups performed about equally well (Sharan et al., 1980).

Group investigation is intellectually ambitious. Students play the role of creative research scholars. In order to achieve these goals, they must work together closely. Good group process is insured in various ways: building commitment to the group and its project, use of division of labor, and group process skills. The developers admit that not every student can be integrated into such a demanding group. They suggest that there are some students not suitable for such collective tasks who perhaps should be allowed to work on their own. Other students may be allowed to shift groups if serious problems of commitment develop. The teacher must work as an intellectual leader and resource person, assisting the groups to develop the more challenging questions and learning tasks, helping the groups with the resources and skills they will need to carry out their tasks, worrying about coordination of the different project groups, and paying close attention to what will be the overall intellectual integration of the curriculum unit. At the same time the teacher must be skillful in assisting groups to overcome their problems, without intervening and telling them directly what decision they must make, or without telling individuals how they should handle interpersonal difficulties in the group.

# 7 The Teacher's Role: Letting Go and Teaming Up

Groupwork changes a teacher's role dramatically. No longer are you a direct supervisor of students, responsible for insuring that they do their work exactly as you direct. No longer is it your responsibility to watch for every mistake and correct it on the spot. Instead, authority is delegated to students and to groups of students. They are in charge of insuring that the job gets done, and that classmates get the help they need. They are empowered to make mistakes, to find out what went wrong, and what might be done about it.

This does not mean that you have given up your position as an authority in the classroom. On the contrary, you are the authority who sets up all the directions for the task; you assign students to groups; you set down the rules; you train the students to use norms for cooperation; you delegate authority to those students who are to play special roles; and, most important, you hold the groups accountable for the product of their work. All this means that when the groupwork starts, you must let go and allow the groups to do their work. This chapter discusses just what letting go means for your role while groups are operating.

Groupwork is better done with the aid of a colleague or some other adult; working alone is much harder for a number of reasons. Designing and evaluating groupwork tasks is a classic case of creative problem solving where "two heads are better than one." Considering that teachers have responsibility for their own classrooms and are not free, let alone welcome, in other teachers' classrooms, you may feel that this is an impractical recommendation. Solving this problem is the second topic of this chapter.

## DELEGATING AUTHORITY

When you stand in front of the class and instruct the students as a whole, when you give out individual seatwork and walk around the classroom overseeing performance, when you divide up the class into reading groups and sit with one group while they take turns reading aloud or answering your questions, you are using direct supervision. Even when, in preparation for groupwork, you gather the class together and provide an orientation, you are using direct supervision.

When groupwork is underway, however, and groups are working and talking together, using the instructions you have prepared, then your authority has been delegated.

### An Effective Management System

Teachers are always surprised to discover how smoothly students can operate on their own in properly designed groupwork. What is the secret of successful management of such complex instruction? The secret lies in clarity—the students' perfect understanding of how they are supposed to behave, what they are supposed to be doing, and where they can turn for help if problems develop. The same is true for a traditional classroom; the difference is simply that with groupwork students have to take more responsibility for their own behavior and for the behavior of others in their group. They should not be turning to the teacher for constant direction, evaluation, and assistance; they should use their peers instead.

Clarity is attained by having as simple a system as possible. Much of the clarity is achieved by training in advance for roles and for cooperation, as well as by the careful planning process recommended in the preceding chapters. All these management techniques operate to control student behavior in a constructive and productive manner without telling students what to do directly. There is no need to control individual students' behavior with systems of points or rewards; the teacher's job is to make the groups and the instructions operate to solve any discipline problems that arise.

The steps for developing such a management system are briefly summarized below.

1. Cooperative norms need to be taught as recommended in Chapter 4 so that students will know how they ought to behave and will act to enforce these behaviors on others.
2. Students should know which group they are in and where that group is supposed to be meeting; a minimum amount of time should be wasted in getting across this vital information.
3. Public and specific information as to who is to play what role and what specific behaviors are expected should be available as described in the previous chapter.
4. Each group should have clear instructions for the task available to them as they work; this will do much to prevent students from having to turn to you as a source of knowledge.
5. Students should have heard a good, brief orientation from you on the objectives of this task and on the criteria for evaluation.

For many groupwork situations, these five considerations will be quite sufficient for everything to go smoothly. In cases where students have had no experience with groups whatsoever, when the class is considered volatile and difficult to control even with traditional, direct supervision, when many different groups are doing very different and complicated activities, or when the group projects are long term, you may want to select a small set of fundamental rules and keep these posted. For example, in our *Implementation Manual* (Navarrete et al., 1985) for the bilingual curriculum on thinking skills, *Finding Out/Descubrimiento*, we recommend the use of the following basic rules:

You MUST COMPLETE each activity and worksheet.

Play your role in the group.
You have the right to ask anyone else in your group for help.
You have the duty to assist anyone who asks for help.
EVERYBODY HELPS. (p. 16)

## The "No Hovering" Rule

You have now delegated authority to groups to carry out
their task. It is of critical importance to let them make decisions *on their own*. They even need to make some mistakes on
their own. They are accountable to you for their work. You
must let go and allow the groups to work things through without your overseeing every step. They must learn to solve some
problems for themselves.

Teachers in traditional classrooms, when they are not lecturing, are spending the bulk of their time getting the students through various tasks. They are showing and telling how
to do the assignments. They are redirecting students who appear to be disengaged from their work. They are answering
many questions that come from individual students.

This kind of direct supervision will undermine the management system you have worked so hard to develop. If you
are available to solve all the problems, students will not rely on
themselves or on their group. Because of their past experiences with supervision, whenever students see you hovering
nearby, they will stop talking to each other and look to you for
direction. That is why teachers have to make a conscious effort not to look as if they were an available member of the
group.

## While the Groups Work

Students are now doing many of the things you ordinarily
do—like answering each other's questions, keeping each other
engaged in the task, helping each other to get started. After
teachers discover that they do not appear to be needed because everything is running without them, they often ask,
"What am I supposed to be doing?"

Actually, you are now free for a much higher level and

more demanding kind of teacher role. You now have a chance to observe students carefully and to listen to the discussion from a discreet distance. You can ask key questions to stimulate a group that is operating at too low a level; you can provide feedback to individuals and to groups; you can stimulate their thinking; and you can reinforce rules, roles, and norms in those particular groups where the system is not operating at its best.

There is a fine line between direct supervision and the supportive role. Direct supervision is standing over students and helping them do their task, answering their questions, and instructing them. In contrast, the supportive supervisor stands well back from the group so that she can hear what is going on without signalling the group that she wants to communicate with them. She speaks with them only if a critical opportunity arises.

More specifically, how would you work as a supportive supervisor?

- A group has "gotten stuck" on a problem and doesn't seem to be getting anywhere. The level of frustration is rising. You ask a few open-ended questions in an attempt to redirect the group discussion. You suggest that the group deal with your questions in their own deliberations—and you walk off.
- A group is not sharing materials cooperatively. You could ask them to stop for a few moments and talk over how they are doing on some of the cooperative norms (ideally, these are prominently posted somewhere in the room). Then you can ask them to have a brief discussion and to tell you what their conclusions are and what they think they should do about it. (Don't stay to supervise the discussion.)
- You see that a group, after considerable trial and error, has solved a difficult problem. You might intervene at that point to tell them how well they have done to persist in the face of failure and that you like the way they have used thorough discussion and creative problem solving to achieve final success.
- A group of second graders has plunged into the task without reading the instructions. You might tell the group that

you don't want them to touch the materials until they can tell you just what they are supposed to be doing. You might say that you are going to return to the group and ask any member to explain what it is they are supposed to be doing. If that person can explain, then they can get started with the materials. Otherwise, they will have to continue to read and discuss.

• One group has finished its task very quickly and is looking around for something else to do. You might open up the task once more by asking some questions about analyzing the problem further or about generalizing the task to another situation. Most of the groupwork tasks should be sufficiently rich so that it will be possible for you to extend the activity in this way.

• One student approaches you with a question about procedure. This question is really answerable from the task instructions. You tell the student to return to the group and find out if anyone else knows the answer to the question from a study of the task instructions. Many teachers allow only the facilitator to approach the instructor with questions, further specifying that this is not to take place until the group is sure that no one knows the answer.

• After conferring with other group members, the facilitator approaches you with a challenging question concerning the substance of their research. You suggest a reference book; this book is available in the classroom because you have thought ahead and have consulted the librarian about what books might be useful.

In none of these examples is the teacher using direct supervision. Instead, she is opening up new kinds of thinking through the use of questioning. She is giving feedback to groups on their use of group process. She is forcing the group back upon its own resources—to take more responsibility for its own learning and functioning. The teacher has become a supportive person and a resource person. A comparison of the differences between direct and supportive supervision is given in Figure 7.1.

FIGURE 7.1: A Comparison of the Behaviors Used in Direct and Supportive Supervision

| *Direct Supervision* | *Supportive Supervision* |
| --- | --- |
| Lecturing and instructing | Giving feedback |
| Telling students how to do task | Redirecting group with |
| Disciplining |     questions |
| Getting students back on task | Encouraging group to solve its |
| Working with one group |     own problems |
| Recitation | Extending activity |
| Monitoring seatwork | Encouraging thinking |
| Leading discussion | Managing conflict |
| | Observing students |
| | Supplying resources |

## Management of Conflict

Some conflict between group members is inevitable and should not be taken as a sign of failure. Nor should it be an opportunity for you to intervene and take over the reins immediately, acting as arbiter, juror, and judge. What can you do?

Ask the group what seems to be the difficulty. Then ask them to think of some alternative strategies for handling the conflict. Even younger students are able to develop workable strategies for managing conflict when challenged to do so.

If the problem seems to be one created by a particularly difficult student, take some systematic notes about that student. Exactly how is he or she behaving? How does the group respond to that behavior? What interests, needs, and strengths do you think that student exhibits? With these notes you can take the time to think up some alternative strategies for dealing with this student. What student would work well with him or her? Instead of allowing the child to be seen purely as a problem, what strengths can you capitalize on? What role might he or she be assigned in the next group session? Instead of disciplining the student yourself, make the system take care of the difficulty.

If the problem is due to a volatile combination of students, make a note not to put that combination together again. Changing the composition of groups on a regular basis and rotation of roles will help to defuse interpersonal problems so that the conflict does not become chronic. If, however, you think you are seeing the same problem in a number of groups, there may be a difficulty in the way you have prepared the students or in the nature of the task. Take the time to have a whole-class discussion during wrap-up and see if you can locate the general problem. Be prepared to make adjustments in your task, to do some retraining and reinforcing of rules and roles, or to develop some strategies with the class as a whole that will solve the problem.

## Orientation and Wrap-up

During orientation you are clearly in direct charge of the students. Their job is to listen and to ask questions if they do not understand. This does not mean that a long lecture is in order. I often stand at the back of the classroom while teachers give orientations and usually note that students have difficulty paying close attention to what the teacher is saying. Even in high school, they seem to "tune out" after five minutes.

Those teachers who use visual aids and who involve the students in a discussion concerning what they are about to experience are much more successful in holding the class's attention than those who attempt to tell everything that the students will need to know. If the students need to develop considerable substantive knowledge before they can carry out the group task, it may be wise to develop a separate lesson on these materials the day before the groupwork. Elaborate preparation for interpersonal and role skills should not be included in the orientation either. In other words, the most common mistake is to try to place too great a burden on the orientation, often making it too lengthy, without analysis of which components can be done in advance and which components can be left to the written instructions or to student discovery.

Wrap-up is an essential stage of groupwork in which the teacher is often in charge. Students have typically been given the authority to make presentations of some kind, so that the class as a whole can share what each group has learned. This is a major opportunity for the teacher to provide specific feedback to groups and to individuals who are making presentations on behalf of their groups. It is a priceless opportunity to offer public praise to students who have done very well in the context of groupwork—particularly those who are not high achievers in conventional academic tasks. This public feedback should be honest, sincere, and sufficiently specific so that students know exactly what they have done well.

Following student presentations, the teacher would do well to comment on what has been learned from this exercise. This is also a good time to comment on how well the group proccss has gone and to discuss with the class how this could be improved in the future. After the students have completed such a vivid experience, your comments will have far greater power to educate than when they follow typical classroom patterns of lecture and recitation.

## WORKING AS A TEAM

One of the most gratifying experiences for a teacher is to plan and carry out groupwork designs with a trusted colleague. Just as students use each other as resources in groupwork, teachers can do the same. With the joint wealth of past experience as to what tasks work well with students and as to how instructions can be made clear, teachers can be highly creative as they work together. They can also provide honest and constructive feedback as ideas develop.

When instruction is complex, as is the case with groupwork, having teachers work together means that they are able to be of great assistance to each other while the class is operating. Perhaps one teacher can stop to work with a group needing feedback, while another keeps an eye on the classroom as a whole. One teacher can prepare the orientation while another can do the wrap-up. The labor of preparing complex materials for learning centers can also be divided.

Another advantage of a colleague is the benefit that accrues when two or more teachers hold formal, scheduled meetings. In these meetings (even if they are as short as twenty minutes) one has a chance to consider various problems that have come up, to raise possible alternatives, to choose one, and to talk once more in the next meeting about how good the decision was. This kind of thoughtful and evaluative decision making is very difficult to carry out all by oneself. In research with teachers, Intili and I have repeatedly found that teachers who hold regular team meetings are better able to implement complex and sophisticated instruction than those who rely on brief huddles just before and during class (Intili, 1977; Cohen & Intili, 1982).

The last major advantage of working with a colleague lies in having someone to make an observation and systematic evaluation of your groupwork in progress. It is almost impossible to run groupwork and evaluate what is happening at the same time. Chapter 9 includes a number of simple techniques for a colleague to use in helping to evaluate your groupwork. Even beginning teachers can provide helpful feedback using these techniques. And you can return the favor by observing in your colleague's classroom.

## Finding Ways to Team

There are two kinds of teaming; one requires more organizational change than the other. The first kind is joint teaching where your colleague actually teaches jointly with you in your classroom. I use the word "colleague" because this person does not necessarily have to be another classroom teacher. I have worked with highly successful teams made up of a resource teacher working with a classroom teacher for one period a day, a teacher and an aide, or a teacher and a trained parent volunteer. If your class is difficult to control and unused to groupwork, you will need another person, especially at the beginning. If your tasks are complex, such as using different science experiments at different learning centers or working with sophisticated equipment like movie cameras, and if you have different groups doing very different tasks, another person becomes a necessity. This is as true for classrooms as it is for any other organization: complex technology is more effective when staff work more closely together (Perrow, 1961).

If you have a friend on the faculty with whom you would like to try some of these groupwork activities, talk to the principal about finding ways to work together. If a large room such as a multipurpose room is free, it is possible to combine two classes for the actual groupwork. If the classes are from different grades, you will be surprised to see how well students of different ages can work together in this setting. If you are going to combine age groups, it is especially important to pick a task that older students can extend and develop but also one that younger students will be able to manage with assistance. It will then also be necessary to include special training to show students how to help without doing each other's work.

If you decide to work with an aide or a volunteer, take the time to train that person as to your expectations of them during the teaching process. If you do not train them, the result will be that they will move in and try to supervise groups directly. Aides or volunteers can become valuable colleagues if you allow them to bring in suggestions and to make evaluations of what is happening. In these circumstances, you are still the decision maker; it is the role of your assistant to observe and gather data about what the problems are during the course of groupwork. You also expect that they will make constructive suggestions during team meetings.

If you cannot manage joint teaching, the next best thing is teaming for planning and evaluation purposes. It is not difficult to find the time for brief meetings with a colleague for planning purposes. In addition, you need to find time for that colleague to visit your classroom and time when you can return the favor. It is during these visits that the evaluation devices can be used. Following evaluation, a meeting should take place to discuss the results of the evaluation and decide what should be done in order to improve the procedures. Most principals are supportive of this type of collegial effort to improve instruction. Some principals even volunteer to take over classes for an hour while the visits are going on. I have worked at very few schools where the teachers and administrators were unable to work out a suitable plan.

Collegial interaction of this sort is highly rewarding. Evaluations of in-service programs requiring this kind of collegial interaction have consistently revealed that teachers find working with a colleague in planning, observation, and evaluation one of the most satisfying and stimulating of their professional experiences. Despite initial doubts about having another teacher watch them at work, they find that constructive criticism from a colleague who is facing the same kind of practical classroom problems is helpful; they realize that they have wanted and needed this kind of feedback for a long time.

# 8 Treating Expectations for Competence

It is time now to return to the dilemma of groupwork discussed in Chapter 3. What have we done about the problem of high status students dominating interaction and of low status students withdrawing from the group? There is an even more fundamental question: Have we done anything to change low expectations for competence, the underlying cause of nonparticipation by low status students?

Recall that high status students are generally expected to do well on new intellectual tasks and low status students are generally expected to do poorly on these same tasks. When the teacher assigns a groupwork task, general expectations come into play and produce a self-fulfilling prophecy in which the high status students talk more and become more influential than the low status students. The net result of the interaction is that the low status students are once again seen as incompetent. This occurs even if groups are given a rich new task that does not stress ordinary academic skills.

Two strategies will have some impact on this problem: (1) Establishing cooperative norms such as "everyone participates" and "everyone helps" will prevent high status students from dominating and will encourage low status students to participate and talk; and (2) Giving every student a part or a role to play will produce participation and verbal behavior from low status students and will prevent high status students from doing all the talking.

Use of these strategies will do much to equalize the interaction between students of different statuses. Furthermore, low status students will improve their performance, just by talking and working together with other students.

Doesn't that take care of the whole status problem? Not exactly—nothing has happened to change expectations for competence. Imagine a well-trained group with different students playing different roles; the low status students are doing just as much talking, on the average, as the high status students. Nevertheless, members of the group still think of the low status students as having fewer and poorer ideas than the high status students. The low status students may be active, but they are still less influential than the high status students. And the low status students still feel that their contributions to the group are less valuable and less competent than the contributions of the high status students. Furthermore, in moving from the successful group experience to other groupwork tasks there will be no improvement in expectations for competence.

In order to produce active behavior in low status students that will be perceived as competent, and in order to produce expectations for competence that will transfer to other tasks, something must be done to change the nature of those expectations for competence. They are too uniform, and too consistently negative. You must find a way to create some positive expectations for intellectual competence that will combine with the preexisting set of negative expectations.

It is possible to design groupwork that will attack the problem of consistently low expectations for intellectual competence. If you are successful in doing so, students who have been unsuccessful in your classroom can acquire a sense of competence that will be acknowledged by their classmates. As you proceed to different groupwork tasks, students can expect themselves and can be expected by their classmates to make good contributions to each new assignment.

## MAKING A LOW STATUS STUDENT THE GROUP EXPERT

One obvious way to change low expectations for competence is to design a situation where the student who is expected to be incompetent will actually function as an expert. The simplest and probably the safest way to do this is to find a task where the student is already an expert. An example might be a Spanish-speaking child who could teach classmates a song or a poem in Spanish. Even this fairly obvious strategy requires careful analysis. Do not assume that because a student has a Spanish surname or speaks some Spanish, he or she knows how to teach something in Spanish. Proficiency in Spanish may be limited; in addition, teaching someone else is a separate skill from knowing how to recite a poem or sing a song. You must prepare the student carefully for this teaching role.

Speaking in Spanish is a kind of expertise that everyone, rightly or wrongly, expects Hispanic students to have. This is a narrow and specific expectation for competence, almost like a stereotype. It is unlikely that the experience of being an expert in Spanish will change expectations for competence on other kinds of tasks because it is a stereotypic expectation associated with ethnicity. A similar situation would be a female who demonstrates expertise in cooking or a black who demonstrates expertise in basketball. Although people are willing to grant females and blacks expertise in these two areas, the expectations for competence *do not transfer* to other valued tasks.

Despite these limitations, a narrow brand of expertise has some merit if it gives the low status child a chance to play the leadership role of teacher. However, unless you point out to the class that the act of teaching the class is a special kind of competence and that it is an important skill, the group will never notice that "teaching the Spanish song" is a different skill from "singing the song."

Every student in your class is an expert in some valued intellectual skill. Try and find out what these are. Rich groupwork tasks allow you to see skills and talents that ordinary classroom assignments never permit. I have seen classrooms with a list of the areas in which each student in the class is listed as an expert. Take note of areas of expertise and find ways to allow different children, particularly those with low academic, social, or peer status, to function as experts in a group. This simple technique is workable as long as the members actually believe that the student is an expert and as long as the student is truly competent.

## EXPECTATION TRAINING

Along with my graduate students and colleagues, I have carried out a number of experiments where expectations were treated by having the low status student become a teacher of a high status student on a new, challenging, and valued task. This method of treatment is called "Expectation Training." Tasks for expectation training are not culturally specific or stereo-typed for any group. We have used tasks like constructing a model from straws based on a mathematical law, building a two-transistor radio, or solving a plastic Chinese puzzle.

The strength of the treatment lies in the way that it at-tacks expectations for competence held by the low status student for himself as well as those held by the high status student for the low status student's performance. Theoretically, mak-ing low status students experts on a new task and making them teachers of that task provides two new sources of positive ex-pectations for competence. The students derive positive ex-pectations from displaying competence on the task itself; in addition, they derive expectations for competence from being successful teachers. These new expectations combine with the older set of negative expectations; the net effect is to raise the general level of expectations for competence. The result is im-proved participation and influence on new group tasks.

In laboratory settings, expectation training has consis-tently produced an increase in participation and influence of children with low social status; treated groups exhibit a pat-tern of equal status behavior. The treatment has worked for black-white groups (Cohen & Roper, 1972); for Chicano-An-glo groups (Robbins, 1977); for Canadian Indian-Anglo groups (Cook, 1974); and for Western and Eastern Jews in Israel (Cohen & Sharan, 1980).

In a field experiment with an interracial summer school, we were able to show that if expectation training was used the first week, it was possible to maintain equal status interaction for six weeks. The black children taught the white children a series of academic and nonacademic tasks. For this purpose, the black children came to the summer school a week early for special training in their role as teachers. At the end of the program, black children were as active and influential, if not more active and influential, than white children on the standard group task of Shoot the Moon (Cohen, Lockheed, & Lohman, 1976). The black children were from a markedly lower social class than the white children in this field study. (All the children were fifth and sixth graders.) However, in the summer school setting the curriculum did not require conventional school skills as a prerequisite to success on tasks in the curriculum.

Expectation training is an extraordinarily powerful treatment. The low status student not only displays an impressive competence but is in a position to direct the behavior of the high status student as does every teacher—a rare opportunity for someone on the bottom of the classroom status order. Even with a nonacademic task (such as a Chinese puzzle) for expectation training, the favorable evaluations received as a puzzle solver and as a teacher will transfer to a wide variety of groupwork tasks requiring intellectual skills.

Expectation training should never be undertaken without serious thought and should not be tried at all if the teacher does not have the resources (aides, older students, volunteers) to spend time with each low status child who will play the role of teacher. The danger is that if you allow the low status child to *fail* as a teacher, you will have knowingly exposed that student to another overwhelming negative evaluation. *This must not be allowed to happen*. The only way to avoid it is careful individualized coaching, so that you are sure that the student is highly confident and can demonstrate his or her competence to the trainer's satisfaction before going on to teach.

Expectation training is not the most practical of classroom treatments. Teachers often do not have the time to prepare students for their role as teacher so that a successful performance is guaranteed. Even if an aide is assigned this task, the aide will need to be carefully trained so that each child reaches some specific criterion level of competence before any demonstration of teaching skills takes place.

One of the most difficult things to achieve in this or any

other kind of status treatment is to convince the low status persons of their competence. It is actually harder to change expectations these students hold for themselves than it is to change expectations classmates hold for them. You may observe that low status students can carry out the task and teach it with considerable skill. But you would be surprised to realize that these students still do not see themselves as skillful.

Another important problem may arise in having the aide do the training. If the teacher belongs to a high status ethnic or racial group, and the aide belongs to the same minority group as the low status students, expectation training may be ineffective. Experimental results have shown that expectation training will *not* produce the desired effects in settings where the adults mirror the status order of the outside society, for example, in a classroom where an Anglo teacher is the "boss" and a Hispanic aide is clearly a subordinate. Unless the aide and the teacher model equal status behavior, the low status student is unlikely to speak up and tell the high status student what to do (Robbins, 1977; Cohen, 1982).

## THE MULTIPLE ABILITY STRATEGY

The "Multiple Ability" treatment is an alternative way to treat expectations for competence in the classroom that is safer and more practical. This strategy changes expectations for competence for a particular groupwork task by convincing the students that many different abilities will be necessary for successful group performance. Furthermore, students understand that no one person will be good at all these abilities and that each person will be good on at least one ability. Each student expects to be competent on at least one of the abilities and not so competent on some of the other abilities required for the new tasks. Because all students possess some favorable expectations for making a contribution to the group, sharp differences in perceived competence and participation between high and low status students are greatly reduced.

## Research Evidence

The multiple ability treatment was originally developed by J. Tammivaara (1982) in a laboratory study of students selected on the basis of having high and average estimates of their own reading ability. Before the students in her experimental groups set to work to solve the survival problem of Lost on the Moon (see Hall, 1971), they were informed that many different abilities were important to a good group solution. Relevant abilities included "listening carefully to what other people have to say," "thinking of new and original uses for objects," and "getting the group to move forward on their task" (Tammivaara, 1982, p. 216). The host experimenter said: "No one person will be good at all these abilities, but each person will be good on at least one" (p. 216). Furthermore, they were told that reading had no relevance to this particular task since all the objects were pictured on cards.

The control groups had no such introduction; they were simply given instructions for the survival problem. After this experience, all groups played the standard game. Those groups that had heard the multiple ability introduction showed equal status behavior, while the others showed a pattern of dominance by the high ability readers. This study demonstrated that one can effectively interfere with status processes by defining multiple abilities as relevant to a task, thereby preventing students from assuming that academic status will be the only relevant basis for predictions of competence.

Rosenholtz (1985) created a one-week multiple ability curriculum in a school where all the children were white and English-speaking but came from a wide range of social class backgrounds. The curriculum was divided into daily one-hour sessions. Students were fourth graders who had known each other for some time and who had had many opportunities to make evaluations of each other on reading ability.

The multiple ability curriculum offered a series of tasks as representative of three different abilities. The curriculum explicitly taught an important general lesson: There are many human abilities that children and adults use in solving problems in life. The three abilities Rosenholtz selected as examples were visual thinking, reasoning, and intuitive thinking. In each case, she showed a film strip of how people use each of these intellectual abilities to solve problems. Following this, the children were assigned to heterogeneous groups. They were told that they were about to carry out a task that used the ability under discussion.

One adult sat with each group to explain the games and to make sure that each student had an experience that ranged from satisfactory to successful. These tasks were carefully engineered so that high ability readers could not dominate and low ability readers would gain more favorable evaluations of their competence. This was accomplished by having students take turns at guessing the answers and by using tasks where everyone contributed something different to the final product.

The game Guess My Rule was developed by Rosenholtz for this curriculum (see Appendix A for a description of the game). It is an example of reasoning ability, a task requiring turn-taking. Because a student can only guess the rule when he or she has a turn, it is impossible for one child to dominate this game and for another child to be left out.

One task used in the series on visual thinking is a good example of division of labor, another strategy to prevent domination. Each student held a 4″ × 1″ × 1″ block of wood. On each long, flat surface was glued one fifth of a Snoopy picture. The children could not show each other their pieces. The adult held one of the blocks and started by describing her part of the picture on one side of the block. This gave the group the cue as to which side of their blocks was part of the picture. They each, in turn, described their blocks until it became clear whose block belonged where in the picture. When a group member thought he or she had it figured out, that student would put down a block in place until the picture appeared, all assembled.

Groups were recomposed with new members after each task so that a wide variety of classmates worked together. In order to see if new, more favorable evaluations had developed for low ability readers, students individually rated their own ability at reasoning, visual thinking, and intuitive thinking. There were very few negative self-evaluations; the range was from "average" to "superior." The self-ratings of high ability readers on the new abilities were no higher than those of the low ability readers.

The second measurement of effect was the standard game of Shoot the Moon. In the results, the low ability readers who had experienced the curriculum were significantly more active and influential on the new task than the low ability readers of the preliminary study (see Chapter 3), who were untreated. Behavior did not truly reflect equal status in treated groups in that there was still a tendency for high ability readers to be more active and influential. But the advantage of the high ability readers was greatly reduced by the treatment.

The multiple abilities curriculum provided low status students with the opportunity to develop favorable self-evaluations and to be evaluated favorably by peers in the context of tasks defined as requiring new and different abilities—tasks where division of labor and turn-taking prevented status phenomena from operating. Once the favorable evaluations had been formed, they combined with the old set of expectations for competence and modified the status effects on a new and different task.

## The Three Steps of a Multiple Abilities Strategy

It is neither difficult nor expensive for an instructor to use a multiple abilities strategy in an ongoing class. It does require rethinking the skills and abilities necessary for the groupwork task. Unless the teacher believes that multiple abilities are called for by the task, he or she will be unsuccessful in using this strategy. Furthermore, special steps should be taken to ensure that the low status students develop favorable expectations for competence on the new abilities. The steps of a practical version of this strategy are outlined below.

*Phase I: Orientation.* Discuss the different abilities that you and the class think will be important. Students must perceive that there are many different dimensions of competence. Convince the class that it is not really possible for one person to be good at all these abilities and that, surely, everyone could do well on at least one. Although it may seem awkward, it is very effective to use an adaptation of Tammivaara's (1982, p. 216) wording, "Everyone will be good on at least one of these abilities; no one will be good at all of them." You do not have to say that reading is irrelevant. Simply mention that reading (or any other conventional academic skill) is one important ability. After describing the task have the students suggest abilities that they think will be important.

*Phase II: During Groupwork.* Observe students carefully, particularly students who you suspect have consistently low expectations for competence. When one of these students performs well at one of the abilities that have been discussed, give immediate, specific, and public recognition for this competence. This will help to ensure the formation of favorable evaluations.

*Phase III: Wrap-up.* Discuss how different students displayed different abilities and, if possible, have a low status student demonstrate for the class as a whole what you saw he or she could do so well.

## What Are Multiple Abilities?

Use of the multiple abilities strategy means thinking in a new way about human intelligence. Instead of thinking about how intelligent or unintelligent a student is, imagine that there are different kinds of intelligence or intellectual abilities that are called forth in different kinds of situations and for different aspects of a given task. Take, for example, the task of teaching. Teaching requires great interpersonal intelligence, organizational ability, conventional academic ability, verbal ability, as well as creative ability.

When you think about the adult world of work, it is comparatively easy to see that many different kinds of abilities are essential to any job such as that of teaching. Yet somehow when we think about intelligence among students, we automatically narrow our thinking to conventional academic criteria—being good at reading, writing, and computing. That narrowness is, in part, a reflection of the narrowness of school curricula. Instead of reflecting the way adults use their minds, school curricula reflect a traditional conceptualization of what is to be learned in school.

In schools, being intelligent at schoolwork is thought of in a unidimensional fashion. One is either good, average, or "no good" at school tasks. Furthermore, one of the earliest indicators of the child's academic ability is his or her ability in reading. Reading ability becomes an index of general intelligence in many classrooms for both students and teachers.

The multiple ability approach is in line with current work on reconceptualizing human intelligence. For a long time human intelligence has been thought of as unidimensional; it could be characterized by a single number; people (and whole races) could be ranked from gifted to stupid. Stephen Jay Gould in his important book *The Mismeasure of Man* (1981) has done the field of education a great service by tracing the history of this idea to its roots, deep in Western culture. His analysis of biases in early and present-day research on the concept of intelligence raises fundamental doubts as to whether we can continue to think of intelligence as unidimensional. Howard Gardner in his book *Frames of Mind* (1983) attempts to reconceptualize human intelligence as multiple and rooted in specific areas of the brain. He distinguishes linguistic, musical, logical-mathematical, spatial, bodily-kinesthetic, and personal intelligences.

There is no official list of multiple abilities. It is a new way of looking at something we have known all along—that we use our intelligence in many different kinds of ways to solve problems and to accomplish important tasks in work and family life. Keep in mind that adults engage in highly complex problem solving as part of their daily lives. Some of these activities are academic, others are technical or political, and many are interpersonal, social tasks. Examples of such adult activities are managing, coordinating, taking the role of the other, teaching, learning, researching, directing, supervising, writing, drawing, building, developing, investigating, negotiating, evaluating, counting, calculating, and acting. These are all activities you can find in rich groupwork tasks.

In order to use the multiple ability approach one must first pick a rich task that requires many different abilities rather than a convergent, "right answer" task. Reading and writing can be two important skills, but students should not have to be able to do these things well in order to make a contribution. Instead, those students who have these skills can assist those who have difficulties.

Chapter 5 recommends that all tasks for groups be sufficiently rich and varied that different students can make different contributions. A narrow task is a paper-and-pencil task that only requires skills such as comprehension, reading, and writing. A rich task uses multiple media and requires a far greater range of intellectual skills.

With the caution in mind that these examples are not to be taken as the preferred list of human abilities, let me make a few suggestions. A teacher of English literature might create a group task of interpreting the motives of a main character; relevant abilities might include understanding why people behave the way they do, going over the text with great care to glean additional clues, and finding a good way to phrase the group's answer. Manipulative science tasks are easily seen as requiring multiple abilities such as observation, precise manipulation, careful data recording, hypothesizing causes and effects, and writing up the report clearly and concisely. In social studies many assignments lend themselves to a multiple ability definition because they involve visual, interpretive, reasoning, and artistic skills; examples of such assignments include building models and drawing maps. Make the abilities specific to the situation in which they will be used, but be sure that they will be seen as important and valuable. Also, do not forget the interpersonal skills that make group life possible and effective.

Elementary school children are capable of many adult intellectual activities and can display impressive abilities in reasoning, hypothesizing, and analyzing as long as the materials they are given to work with are familiar and understandable. As a matter of fact, younger children are sometimes better at solving problems than their elders because they are less afraid of making mistakes and are more willing to use trial and error.

Even tennis instruction can be defined as involving multiple abilities. A tennis instructor wanted to avoid having begining students withdraw from his class because they felt they were no good at the sport. He used groupwork to help each group practice different subskills that he carefully defined as separate abilities, such as serving, placing yourself on the court to receive the ball, and use of backhand. When all group members mastered the practice drill of the new skill, they proceeded to teach other groups. Attendance at the tennis class was greatly improved by this multiple ability application of groupwork. More students developed a specific sense of competence and were thus encouraged to continue their participation in class.

Remember that it is not enough to create a rich multiple abilities task—in addition, the teacher must be able to describe the particular abilities required by the task. If you fail to do this, students will assume there is only one ability necessary for successful performance.

## LIMITATIONS

These strategies for treating status problems are highly recommended for groupwork. They will increase engagement and participation of low status students. They will improve expectations for competence in a way that will transfer to new and different group tasks.

There is no reason, however, to expect newly acquired favorable expectations for competence to transfer to reading and math lessons conducted in a traditional fashion. If you want to treat the problem of low general expectations for competence on the part of low status students in such a way that improved effort and engagement will occur in all areas of your curriculum, then you should consider creating a multi-ability classroom. This concept will be discussed in Chapter 11.

# 9 Evaluating Your Engineering

Kathy Egan and Debbie Marsing worked as a team on the first day of groupwork in Ms. Egan's secondary school swimming class. Students were assigned to work in pairs on developing the whip kick for the breast stroke. Students were supposed to help each other by analyzing each other's stroke and by making suggestions for improvement. The task was defined as requiring multiple abilities such as observation skills, ability to analyze your partner's movement, understanding your partner, coordination, strength, and endurance. Ms. Marsing evaluated the groupwork by making general observations, by watching several students whom Ms. Egan had pointed out as having had problems in the class, and by giving the students a simple questionnaire to fill out. Ms. Marsing wrote:

> The instructions to the students were clear. Kathy explained the different tasks involved especially well. Kathy took approximately five to seven minutes to explain the different abilities involved in the task, as well as how the students should work together. She had a chalkboard with the abilities listed and the helper and doer roles that corresponded to that ability.
> In the actual activity, the students in Group 2 had trouble getting started. They were the least involved in the beginning. Both students commented that they knew the breast stroke perfectly. When they began to teach and learn the breast stroke from each other, both students were engaged. . . .
> Another pair, Ray and Rick, were on task during most of class time. During the five minute observation, it appeared that Ray and Rick were working together; however, minimal verbal interchange was heard. They did not deliberate much, but Ray would swim ahead as the doer and Rick would watch. When Ray got back a couple of words may have been spoken, but

then Rick would be on his way, swimming, this time with Ray watching. . . . Ray had some trouble communicating because of his lack of English proficiency. . . . Ray often used his hands to help describe the whip kick to Rick. Rick, who had the worst whip kick, was being helped by Ray, who had a good kick. Here, the lower status student was much needed for his movement and observation skills. He was doing well on these skills notwithstanding his weak English speaking skills.

Based on their performances, it appears that students didn't completely understand the procedure of helping and teaching each other. Gradually, they understood by watching other groups perform the team task. I didn't see the weaker students stand out any more than the others during the class. This also relates back to the third item on the questionnaire. The students who *did* understand were both high and low status students. Also, the students who *didn't* understand were high and low students. Even though some students were primarily the helper or doer, the source of this domination was a function of the students' movement skills rather than their relative status. Those with better skills were helping those who were less skilled. (Egan & Marsing, 1984, pp. 2, 3, 5, 6)

As a result of this evaluation, the teaching team realized that analyzing someone else's performance in swimming was a skill that required special preparation before groupwork begins. Next year Ms. Egan will have this critical piece of information available in her notes when she begins to schedule activities in preparation for groupwork.

Be critical of your groupwork the first time you try it. Even if you have faithfully adhered to the general principles for designing groupwork, principles do not fit concrete situations without adjustment. Even with the best laid plans, there is room for improvement.

Teachers who have designed groupwork carefully are typically so delighted at the capacity of student groups to run themselves on the first trial that they are in no mood to be critical. However, it is extremely important to examine the very first day of operation with an objective eye. Some problems can be observed and corrected quickly; others may require revising the initial instructions or making other structural changes in the way the task is handled. Even if it is too late to correct a problem in a class you are conducting, careful notes will allow you to improve the design for the next class. If, as recommended, you have found a partner who can work with you in planning and evaluation, you can rely on your partner's observations to provide the needed objectivity.

## TOOLS FOR EVALUATION

Some effective and simple tools to use in evaluating your own groupwork are provided below and in Appendix B. These have been developed in classrooms and do not require special training in data collection or analysis. Practicing teachers and beginning teachers have found them practical and useful. Included within this chapter are a sample observation guide and a participation scoring sheet; a sample student questionnaire, along with a guide for analyzing it, is included in Appendix B. The sections below will describe all these forms and how to use them. Depending upon which aspects concern you the most, they may be used separately or together. Undoubtedly you have a number of concerns: Will the students be fully engaged with the groupwork? How well will I be able to play my role? Will the students be able to cooperate? How well will the low status students do? Go over the various instruments and select parts or specific questions of concern. It is more important to focus on a few important aspects of evaluation than to do a superficial job with all possible aspects.

### Guide for an Outside Observer

I am assuming that you will have done some of the initial planning with a partner and that you have arranged for this partner to visit your classroom on the day you plan to get the groupwork started. You have discussed with your partner what you are trying to do, what the problems are, and which students may require special attention. As a result, the plan for evaluation is a joint decision about what and whom to look at.

While the students start to work in their groups, the observer can move around the room watching and listening. If you point out to the observer the students you are most concerned about, she or he can observe their behaviors carefully. These may be low status students, students who lack English proficiency, domineering students, or students who usually present behavior problems. The observer can also watch you in action.

Figure 9.1 presents a Sample Guide for the Observing Teacher. Using these guidelines, the observer can take notes. These are possible questions for the observer. You should go over this guide with the observer in the planning session, picking out which questions you want to include. You may want to add a few others.

Part A focuses on the teacher's orientation. It is particularly important for the observer to arrive in time to see and hear you at this stage. So many problems start with confusion in the orientation. On the other hand, in an effort to make all the details clear, the teacher risks losing the attention of the students by trying to get across too much information in a lecture format.

Part B directs the observer's attention to the groups at work. A good procedure is to look over the whole classroom and count how many students are wandering, unattached to any group, and how many students are waiting for the teacher. The observer should scan the classroom and try to determine how many of the groups seem to be at work on their tasks in the way in which they were supposed to work (Questions 1 and 2). Then the observer can move around to stand near enough to each group to hear and see, but not so near that students become conscious of being observed. Questions 3–7 in Part B should be considered for each group. A seating plan with the groups numbered can enable the observer to share observations on particular groups with the teacher.

Part C has to do with selected students who are seen as problematic in the groupwork setting. It is important to spend about five minutes with each of these students taking notes on the questions for each one.

Part D deals with you, the teacher. The first three questions are on common problems that teachers have when they

FIGURE 9.1: Sample Guide for the Observing Teacher

## A. ORIENTATION

1. How clear are the instructions?

2. Does the instructor make use of visual aids and discussion rather than lecturing?

3. How attentive are the students to the orientation?

4. Is the assignment of facilitator and other roles clear? Do the students know who the facilitators are and what they are supposed to do?

5. Does the instructor make clear that people have the right to ask group members for help—and that group members have the duty to assist others?

6. Is the assignment of students to groups and the locations for groups carried out quickly and efficiently?

7. *For Multiple Ability Tasks*: Does the instructor make explicit the multiple abilities involved in the task? Does he or she make clear that reading and writing are only two of the abilities involved in the task? Does he or she make clear that everyone will be good on at least one of the abilities?

## B. STUDENTS AT WORK IN THEIR GROUPS
*Overview*

1. How many students are wandering around, not part of a group? How many students are waiting for the teacher?

2. How many of the groups are engaged in their task? Are there any groups where students are working individually rather than as part of the group?

*Group by Group*

3. Are the students confused about what they are supposed to do? If so, is the group functioning to solve the problem?

4. *For classes that have received training in cooperation*: Make a list of the cooperative norms included in the training. Do you see evidence of these norms in operation? Do you see situations where the students are failing to observe these cooperative norms? Describe.

5. *For groupwork with specific roles*: Make a list of roles and the expected behaviors. For each role, can you hear and see someone

playing this role in the group? Are there any roles that are not in evidence? Is the facilitator (if there is one) dominating the group?

6. Do you see any evidence of conflict? Describe.

7. Is any one student dominating a group? Is there one student who is saying very little?

## C. SELECTED STUDENTS

The teacher should point out the students he or she wants observed, so that observer can take notes on what is happening to particular students. Prepare a list of these students, and take notes on what is happening to each one.

1. Do some of the weaker students show a grasp of the problem? If they are having difficulty, is someone helping them?

2. Are low status students participating? Is anyone listening to them? If they are supposed to be playing a role, are they doing so?

## D. THE TEACHER

1. Is the teacher hovering over the groups and not allowing them to figure out things for themselves?

2. Is the teacher spending most of the time getting students back on task?

3. Is the teacher spending most of the time trying to help the students with how to do their assignment?

4. When a group or a student has a question, does the teacher try to get the group to solve the problem for themselves?

5. Is the teacher stimulating thinking with specific feedback and questions?

The observer should go through each of the above parts systematically, taking notes in answer to each question that is applicable after spending some time observing the groups, the students, and the teacher.

first start groupwork: hovering over groups in a way that inhibits their interaction; spending too much time trying to keep students on task instead of letting the groups take responsibility; and spending too much time trying to get the students through the task instead of letting the group members help each other.

Even if you do manage to avoid these problems, your chief concern may be the mechanics of getting everyone through the task. Particularly at first, it is very difficult to give good feedback to groups and to ask them stimulating questions to encourage their thinking. This skill may only come with sufficient time and practice. Don't be disappointed if you are not able to play this part of your role at first. The last two questions deal with these aspects of your role. Be sure that the observer takes sufficient time to watch you in action so as to get a fair picture.

## Use of a Student Questionnaire

If the students are at least fourth graders, many important questions can be answered with a questionnaire. If all the students do not read well, you can read the items out loud. A Sample Student Questionnaire is included in Appendix B. These are questions that have been very successful with children as young as nine years. These particular items allow you to examine the success of low status students. By asking students to put down their names on the questionnaire, you can pick out the students of special interest and see whether they reported participating. You can actually see if any low status students were picked as having the best ideas or were chosen as having done the most or least talking in the group. There is usually a good relationship between students' reports of such matters and systematic scoring of an observer.

If you have used a multiple ability strategy, then students should be able to list an ability on which they thought they did well. Also, they should be able to list some of the abilities you introduced in addition to reading and writing.

Even the success of the training in cooperative norms can be checked with a student questionnaire. Do they report experiencing problems with not being listened to or with talking much less than they wanted to? Did people have trouble getting along in the group? Would they be willing to work with this group again? You should pick and choose questions according to your major concerns. You can make up additional questions.

A Guide to Analyzing the Student Questionnaire is also included in Appendix B. The directions should be self-explanatory. This guide is divided by the kinds of questions teachers want answered about their groupwork. Data analyses are suggested that will provide some answers to each question.

## Systematic Interaction Scoring

An alternative to the questionnaire method is systematic participation scoring by an outside observer. This is much less difficult than it sounds. It is relatively easy to obtain a rough estimate of the rates of participation of different students. The observer can spend some time writing down answers to the questions you have provided in the Guide for the Observing Teacher; in a fifty-minute session, there will also be time to do some systematic scoring. In any case, it will be important for you to have everything ready and to have instructed your observer ahead of time in the procedures you want.

Select the "target students" you want to have observed. These may be any or all of the following: students with low academic status; students who tend to dominate; minority students who have little social influence among their classmates; very quiet and nonparticipating students; students with limited English proficiency; and/or students who present special behavioral problems. Next, make out a scoring sheet, such as that shown in Figure 9.2, in which you draw the location of the various groups around the classroom, with a box to represent each student in each group. Point out the location of the target student within the group when the observer is ready to score. Have the observer label the boxes in each group to represent the target students.

The observer should spend at least five minutes scoring each group. I am assuming that there will be five or six groups with four or five students each. The observer simply makes a hatch mark inside the appropriate box for every speech a student makes relevant to the assignment. That speech can be as short as "OK," or it can run for several minutes. A speech ends when the person stops talking, starts talk that is social or un-

FIGURE 9.2: Sample Participation Scoring Sheet

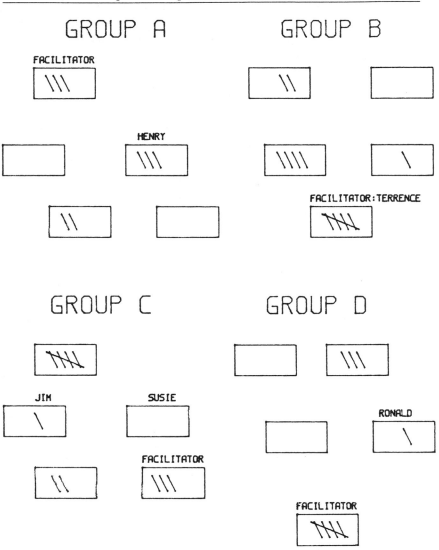

related to the task, or is interrupted by another speaker. It is important to record the contribution of the target student. Sometimes errors will be caused by members of the group moving around and in and out of the group. Try not to let this happen for the target student. If the target student moves away from the group and ceases participating, it should be so noted. The observer has to stand close enough to the group to hear and see, but not so close as to make the students aware of what he or she is doing.

The tabulation and analysis of these data are very simple (see Figure 9.3). How many of the target students were never seen participating? How many students in the whole class were never seen participating? If the target students make up half or more of the nonparticipating students, you are observing a status problem. More precise calculations can be made by examining the number of times the target students were scored in comparison to the number of times other people in their group were scored. The simplest way to do this is to compare the average number of speeches of target students to the average number of speeches for other members of their group (see the second sample calculation in Figure 9.3).

Then compare the target students' figures to the average figure for the group. Are they below average? Are most of the target students below average in their respective groups? If the

FIGURE 9.3: Sample Participation Scoring Calculations

---

*How many of the nonparticipants in the class (i.e., students who never talked) were low status students?*

|   |   |   |
|---|---|---|
| *a.* Total nonparticipants | | 6 |
| *b.* Low status nonparticipants | | 1 |
| Percentage low status ($a \div b \times 100$) | | 17% |

*Conclusion:* Very few of the nonparticipants were low status students.

*How did the rate of target students' participation compare with the average rate of their group?* (Sample calculation given here is for Group A; calculations for other groups should be made in the same manner.)

|   | Target Students | Other Students |
|---|---|---|
| Number of students | 1 | 4 |
| Total number of speeches | 3 | 5 |
| Average speeches per student | 3 | 1.25 |

*Conclusion:* Henry talked more than average for his group.

groupwork task has been effective in moderating status effects, some target students should be below average, some close to average, and some above. This method of scoring also allows you to tell at a glance if some member of a group is dominating the group by talking far more than anyone else. If you are concerned that your facilitators are doing too much of the talking, have the observer note the facilitators on the chart so that you can examine their rate of speaking in comparison to the average rate of other members of the group.

The figures for any single target student should be viewed with caution because it may well be that the particular five minutes that the group was being scored were not representative of the group's pattern of interaction as a whole. This method of scoring has the advantage of objectivity but the disadvantage of allowing only limited conclusions to be drawn from the numbers. The questionnaire has the advantage of richness of the inferences that can be drawn but the disadvantage of the subjectivity of the responses.

## IMPROVING THE GROUPWORK

Schedule a conference with your partner. Congratulate yourself on how well things have gone. What are the major problems that have been identified? These are the agenda items for your conference, and you should take time to think about possible solutions in advance. If your groupwork is ongoing, some of the solutions can be put into practice immediately. Start with the questions identified in the planning session for the evaluation. For example, if you were concerned with the clarity of your instructions, then check all the data you have on this point. After pulling together everything that has been learned from the evaluation, including the systematic data and your own rough observations, come to some conclusions about how the next session of groupwork could be improved. It is very important to do this in a systematic fashion. Your conference will be much more effective if you force yourself to come to some decisions in light of what you have learned. What has gone very well and can be left alone? What needs some adjustment and what do you and your partner think should be done about it? Write down these decisions and file them along with your instructional plans for the groupwork task. If you do not do this, it is too easy to forget what you have learned and to return to reliance on a vague overall judgment of how it went. You are not a good observer when you are trying to do something new and difficult like introducing and running groupwork. Furthermore, there is not much point to going through the motions of a systematic evaluation if you do not pay attention to the data and use it to make decisions.

What can you do if you carry out a status analysis and conclude that you still have a marked status problem, with some students doing most of the work and low status students offering very little to the group? Go back to Chapter 8 and see if there are some techniques you can introduce. Perhaps you need to spend more time with a multiple ability introduction. Perhaps you should observe low status students during groupwork and find a way to praise any contribution they make to the group. Perhaps you need to introduce some new roles that will force everyone to make a contribution.

A teacher cannot become a full-time evaluator. Obviously one has to pick a practical method of evaluation. It makes sense to try one of these techniques at a time. As you gain experience, it takes much less time to analyze the data. If you are attempting to treat a particular problem you have identified from the first round of evaluation and you want to evaluate the second round to see if things have improved, be sure to use the same instruments the second time. When you have tried out the new solutions and evaluated them, you will have a tested groupwork format that you and your partner and any other colleagues can use. You will be surprised to find that a carefully thought out and evaluated design will work well with a wide variety of classes; the students will respond with enthusiasm and excitement year after year.

# 10 Groupwork in the Bilingual Classroom

The dedicated classroom teacher of a bilingual or an English as a Second Language (ESL) classroom faces a scene of enormous complexity—linguistic, academic, and cultural. At the same time as the teacher struggles to help the children understand what is to be done in each assignment, he or she is trying to improve language proficiency and often to remediate basic skills. Furthermore, there are such differences in what each child will need to understand instruction and to make reasonable progress that conventional methods of ability grouping do not really simplify the situation. If the teacher groups children by language proficiency (as has been recommended by the federal government), what does she do with the academic differences? And if she groups by academic ability, how can she be sure that everyone understands the language of instruction?

I am not a specialist in bilingual education, but for the past seven years I have worked with teachers in elementary classrooms where the issue of language is a central one. Early in this work, I discovered that it was not a clear-cut issue of whether the child was Spanish speaking, English speaking, or proficiently bilingual. Very often we find children who do not test as proficient in either English *or* Spanish. The actual linguistic status of such children is not well understood.

Furthermore, the issues of social class and of culture are thoroughly mixed with the issue of language. Some of these children with limited or minimal English and Spanish come from very poor economic conditions; they are arriving at school with the strengths of their own culture but without many of the preschool experiences that prepare children for the typical

128

curriculum. Also from low income homes are some children who have experienced no schooling; it is not uncommon to find new immigrants of eight or nine years of age who have never before been in school.

Many third-, fourth-, and fifth-grade bilingual classrooms contain children with minimal skills in reading and writing any language; some of these students started school with limited English proficiency. They had no access to instruction in a language they could understand; as a result they have not made good academic progress. For those students with proficiency in Spanish but with limited English proficiency, it would seem clear that instruction in the mother tongue in these basic skill areas is critical to insure academic progress. Many of the classrooms that I have been privileged to work with have proficient bilingual teachers and teaching materials in both languages. Children in these settings have the major advantage of having access to the language of instruction.

To make the scene even more complicated, there are other non-English languages in the schools. With the new Asian immigrants come a variety of languages such as Laotian and various Vietnamese dialects. Often it is not possible to find in the classroom another child, credentialed teacher, or trained aide who knows the language of the newcomer. These children are typically placed in ESL classes where the top priority is to learn English quickly, sometimes to the neglect of the other academic subjects.

Most commonly, the school's major goals for bilingual and ESL classes are to increase linguistic proficiency in English and to move students up to grade level in basic skills. (This emphasis on learning English to the exclusion or subordination of the development of competence in Spanish is severely criticized by specialists in bilingual education.) Groupwork offers a powerful tool for the attainment of both these goals. At the same time, it can be used to enable teachers of such classrooms to provide access to higher order thinking skills. This chapter will start with the issue of oral proficiency and will move to the problem of presenting the grade-level curriculum to a class that is heterogeneous academically and linguistically. The final section will illustrate how groupwork can be used to produce broad-gauge achievement results with a bilingual approach designed to develop thinking skills.

## ORAL PROFICIENCY

In a review of the research literature on how children acquire a second language, Neves finds that researchers agree that second-language learners must be exposed to peers who speak that language and that this exposure can influence the kind of language acquired and the speed with which it is acquired (Neves, 1983; Hatch, 1977). However, common school practices work against peer interaction between English-proficient and limited-English-speaking children. In the first place, limited-English-speaking children are often removed from the regular classroom and placed in special classrooms either for bilingual instruction or for ESL. Certainly in this setting, they are unlikely to experience peer interaction with English-speaking classmates. Secondly, within classrooms where there are proficient English speakers, current teaching practices rarely make peer interaction part of formal instruction (Goodlad, 1984). Even within model bilingual classrooms that included English-speaking students, Arias (1983) found that the children were called upon to speak English during recitation, but were mostly very quiet during her observations at other times— limited-English-speaking children had little opportunity to practice English with their peers.

Clearly groupwork represents an excellent opportunity to expose the language learner to peers who speak English. Particularly if the teacher prepares the children so that they will be ready and able to participate, the benefits for growth of oral language will be substantial. What kind of group interaction will be most beneficial for the child who is learning English? Krashen (1981), considered an outstanding authority on second-language acquisition, argues that the child must experience "comprehensible input." Comprehensible input is language that is a bit beyond the learner's current level of proficiency. Simply immersing the child in an English-speaking group may not present comprehensible input at all. However, if the situation provides nonverbal cues and context from manipulative materials or charades, for example, interaction with peers may become comprehensible.

According to Joshua Fishman (1974),

> The learner speaks and listens in interactions in which it is necessary to communicate. If the teacher can create realistic communicative situations in which supporting non-verbal cues exist and in which emphasis is placed on the communicative function or purpose of the interaction, s/he will have gone far toward stimulating the conditions under which successful language learning takes place outside the classroom. (p. 254)

The researchers describe the kind and context of the verbal input that is optimal. Krashen (1982) states that the best input is interesting and relevant. Cazden (1979) suggests that the context is important; activities (such as academic tasks) that children are actively engaged in for nonlanguage reasons are preferable.

These recommendations are very similar to what I have called "rich tasks for groupwork." Particularly if training and the organization of the groupwork have insured that everyone must participate, it would seem that the stage is set for the optimal conditions that the experts recommend.

## Groupwork and the Development of Oral Proficiency

A kindergarten teacher who participated in research in her own classroom as part of the Teacher Investigator Project* was surprised at how easy it was to integrate groupwork into her teaching.

> It was so simple, we didn't realize that it was going to be that simple—we were assuming that it was going to be this tremendous, difficult, complicated thing—and it really wasn't that hard at all. You could adapt a lot of tasks to work in those

---

*The Teacher Investigator Project was financed by the Anglo American Education Fund and conducted under the auspices of the Stanford University School of Education.

kinds of situations. So you can integrate normal daily things like reading and math. It doesn't have to be something you get out of an oral language development book. Once you learn how to give them independence, you can adapt things from the text.

This teacher's class presented typical problems of differences in linguistic proficiency. Many of the children at this school enter kindergarten with a limited vocabulary. Furthermore, this limited vocabulary may be divided between two languages. Some children with limited English proficiency are unwilling to speak in the classroom at all. As one of these children was described, "When he first came and you would ask 'What's your name?' he would just smile." Others in the same class have a good level of proficiency in either Spanish or English.

The issue for this teacher was, How do you get these shy children to talk? Do you try to teach them some more English through whole-group activities such as drill and practice, or through reading out loud to them? And what do you do with those who have a good grasp of English while you are working with those who do not?

With the help of the school's reading teacher, the teacher found that kindergarteners given a pretraining program in activities such as Broken Circles that are designed to help them work as a group were then able to participate in many additional activities that stimulated lively discussions. Examples of such activities included giving each group a card with a new word on it and asking them to develop a charade portraying this word so that other groups could guess it. Here, those children who knew English acted as a valuable resource and explained the word to those who did not. Furthermore, everyone had ideas about how the charade should be carried out. In still another task, the reading teacher came to the room with paper pig ears and noses for each group. Their task was to enact "The Three Little Pigs." According to the teacher's report the children developed numerous adaptations of the original story with a good deal of excitement and maximum communication. This classroom teacher even found that simple tasks requiring visual memory could be adapted to group discussion. She gave them a detailed drawing of an elephant followed by an elephant drawing with many details missing. Each child had to fill in the incomplete version, but they helped each other with the details, for example, "Pedro, you're missing the eye." Before the school year was over this teacher found it relatively easy to have one or two oral proficiency activities a day. Interestingly, when the teacher and the reading specialist compared tape recordings of a group of children discussing a live animal made before and after these experiences, they were pleased and gratified to find that almost all the children had increased dramatically in their willingness and ability to speak.

## Group Composition and Linguistic Proficiency

If the task is rich with context, pictographs, and manipulatives, it is possible to place children who share no common language in the same group. Although it is still quite a struggle for the newcomer, if the group is trained to see that everyone gets the help needed, the children will do a remarkable job of communication.

If at all possible, mixed language groups are preferable. Otherwise the students will not have the benefit of hearing peers with English proficiency. When a child is monolingual in Spanish or in another language, he or she should be combined with English speakers and with a proficient bilingual child. The bilingual child needs to be taught that he or she is a valuable bridge in the group, explaining to the monolinguals what the others are saying and offering special help to the non-English-speaking students. In the classrooms where both languages were utilized by both teachers and children, Neves (1983) found that the bilingual children had, as a whole, the highest social status; they were most often chosen on a sociometric measure as friends and as good in math and science. As the year progresses in a bilingual classroom, one can often find children who can understand another language even though they cannot speak much of it as yet. My staff has often observed conversations between a Spanish- and an English-speaking child, each speaking in his or her own language, but clearly understanding the other.

In the Spanish-English bilingual classroom, sometimes members of a group will speak in Spanish and sometimes they will speak in English. There is no need to enforce an English-only rule; English proficiency will develop in this context. If there are English monolinguals in the group, the rules of co-operation work against excluding the English speaker from understanding what the others are saying. By the same token the Spanish speaker will not be excluded in a predominantly English-speaking group.

## GRADE-LEVEL CURRICULUM IN HETEROGENEOUS SETTINGS

Very often, by the time the limited-English-speaking students reach the fourth or fifth grade, they speak English in the classroom. However, while they were struggling to master the language, they missed instruction in the basic skills and so are functioning several years behind grade level. The most pressing problem experienced by the teacher is the need to remediate basic skills while moving ahead with the grade-level curriculum.

Once the students have been trained to work in groups, curricular tasks that are required for the grade level, tasks with many basic skill components, can be adapted for groupwork. Students who are more advanced can assist those who are less advanced. Students who are bilingual can assist those who do not understand the English text. From the fourth grade up, the new immigrant can receive excellent assistance because there are so many proficient bilingual students. The efficiency of the teacher is multiplied in this way because there are many "assistant teachers" who are making sure that everyone understands the instructions and the text of the assignment.

A fourth-grade teacher and a fifth-grade teacher I worked with in such settings found that they could teach Spanish and English grammar as well as skills of reading comprehension of a very high order by training their students to work in groups and by composing heterogeneous groups. The fifth-grade teacher reported that the students were able to work with eighth- and ninth-grade textbooks in science. She had the groups paraphrase several sentences for every two pages they read. They had to recognize the topic sentence in each paragraph and to underline the key concepts. They used these key concepts to make up their own table of contents for their version of the material. This was a three-month assignment given to groups. She reported that their work came back showing excellent comprehension. The students would help each other with the reading and would then discuss how to complete the assignment. Students played roles of reader, recorder, and facilitator. This is an excellent example of how groupwork can permit the teacher of the heterogeneous classroom to teach to the highest level and not to the lowest common denominator or even to the average student.

## THE "FINDING OUT" APPROACH

*Finding Out/Descubrimiento* (De Avila and Duncan, 1980) is a set of activity cards and worksheets designed to foster the development of thinking skills in second through fifth grades. All learning materials are presented in Spanish, English, and pictographs. The Program for Complex Instruction at Stanford University has developed a system of classroom management that is used in conjunction with these materials (Navarrete et al., 1985). In earlier chapters I have already described some of the key features of cooperative learning developed at Stanford for this instructional approach. Chapter 4 described the cooperative techniques used to prepare heterogeneous groups to work at learning centers. Each child is responsible for completing the task and worksheet, but the group is responsible for seeing that everyone gets the help he or she needs. Chapter 6 described the specific roles such as facilitator, checker, and reporter that take over some of the work of the teacher and insure that no one is left behind or becomes disengaged.

In this chapter I would like to show how the Finding Out approach contributes to the development of oral proficiency, remediation of basic skills, and development of grade-level concepts in math. However, the dramatic gains that we have seen with the Finding Out approach occur *only* when teachers and students receive adequate preparation for a classroom management system that involves extensive training for cooperation, multiple roles for students at the learning center, and delegation of authority by the teacher. The curriculum materials are marvelously engineered, but they are not magic. Unless children have proper access to each other as resources, and unless they are taught to solve problems as a group, many children will not understand what to do with the materials.

## Materials and Management

Finding Out activities use the concepts of science and math to develop thinking skills. At each learning center are two activity cards, one in English and the other in Spanish. The cards tell the students what the activity is and ask them some key questions. There are many challenging words on these cards such as "perimeter," "latitude," and "hexagon." Clearly these words are beyond the reading level of most of the students in second- and third-grade classrooms, where many cannot read or write at all at the beginning of the school year. Cards have pictographs indicating the nature of the activity. There are also worksheets in Spanish and English for each child at the learning center. They often ask the child to describe what happened; they also ask: "Why do you think it happened?" They may require a child to estimate in advance how big something will be. Then they ask him or her to put down the results of actual measurement and how far off this was from the initial guess. In this way the worksheets require a high level of inference and skills such as estimation, while at the same time requiring basic skills such as reading, written expression, and computation.

Measuring, experimenting, constructing, estimating, hypothesizing, analyzing, and many other intellectual activities allow the child to develop strategies for problem solving. The Finding Out activities always involve interesting manipulable materials. They have been developed so that they do not assume that the child has had a rich set of preschool experiences that are relevant to math and science.

Key concepts, such as linear coordinates, are embedded in the activities. The child encounters linear coordinates repeatedly in different forms and at different centers. For example, at one center, students locate their homes on a map, using the coordinates. At another they work with longitude and latitude on a globe. After repeated experience with these abstract ideas in different media, the child acquires a fundamental grasp of the idea that will transfer so that he or she will recognize it in new settings, including in an achievement test.

The group has many functions in this setting. In the first place it is essential to assure that all children have access to the task. Unless they get help in reading the activity card, many of the children will be unable to get the benefit of the activity. Other children who can read perfectly well may still have difficulty with figuring out how a balance scale works or with winding coils in the unit on electromagnetism. Students are supposed to ask each other for assistance; they have experienced specific cooperative games designed to internalize this behavior and the behavior of helping others without doing it for them (see Chapter 4). The facilitator is specifically taught to see to it that everyone gets the help that is needed (see Chapter 4). Both cooperation and the many assigned roles help to insure that each person benefits from the activity.

A second function of the group is to provide a forum where differences in ideas about what to do and about what good answers are can be shared and discussed. The instructions on the activity cards leave a good deal of uncertainty in many tasks. The members of the group have to employ trial and error and must share their results, either by showing each other or by discussion. Again, the children have practiced explaining to each other and showing each other how things work in special exercises (Chapter 4).

A third function of the group is to take care of the problems of children who tend to get frustrated or who often become disengaged. Instead of the teacher having to move around the room to the six learning centers to assist children who are slipping off task, the group functions to make sure that everyone is at work. Unless the task is completed, the group cannot move on to the next center.

A fourth function of the group is to deal with the problem of linguistic differences. The bilingual child explains to the Spanish monolingual what the others are saying. The child who lacks English proficiency is exposed to a rich language experience as he or she uses the vocabulary of the activity card in a situation with all the context and nonverbal cues needed for "comprehensible input." By the same token, the English speakers are receiving input from the Spanish speakers. Instead of the teacher having to explain everything in both Spanish and English, the activity cards, the manipulative materials, and the linguistic resources of the group take care of this problem.

At the start of each Finding Out session, the teacher gives a brief orientation, perhaps demonstrating the concepts from one of the most difficult centers in that unit. The orientation can be a lively demonstration using visual aids and involving active discussion with the students. The teacher is asked to include a multiple ability treatment with a discussion of different kinds of intellectual abilities that will be called for in this set of learning centers. As prescribed in Chapter 8, the teacher includes the motto that no one will be good at all these abilities, but everyone will be good at something. He or she may also talk about the classroom management system, emphasizing norms of cooperation or how she or he wants one of the roles played.

While the students are working at the learning centers, the teaching team (sometimes a teacher and an aide and sometimes two credentialed teachers) circulates around the room, taking care not to interfere with the process of talking and working together. Only the facilitator may be sent to a teacher to ask questions; and even then teachers ask the facilitator to make sure that no one in the group can answer the question. The management system functions to free teachers from spending most of their time keeping students on task and making sure that everyone understands the instructions. Instead of having to be everywhere at once as direct supervisors, they are supportive supervisors. This involves asking higher order questions, stimulating the children's thinking, extending their activities, and giving specific feedback to groups and individuals. Teachers are on the alert for the display of some of the multiple intellectual abilities such as reasoning, visual thinking, and preciseness, especially on the part of low status children. If a teacher observes a low status child performing one of the multiple abilities well, he or she takes the time to give specific and public feedback so that the child knows precisely what was done well.

At the end of each session, there is a wrap-up. The reporter from each learning center may share what the group has discovered. A low status student may provide a special demonstration of what he or she has done at the learning center. The teacher may point out some difficulties that some of the groups are having with particular learning centers. At this point the teacher may undertake an explanation of a scientific concept. Or the teacher may discuss how cooperation and role-playing are proceeding.

The students experience this approach for approximately one hour a day, four days a week. They are repeatedly reading and writing in a context that is highly relevant and interesting for them. Even though they may have to accept help, they want to put their own words down on their worksheets. For example, when children see what happens to the kernel of corn held over a Bunsen Burner in a test tube, they want to write down their own ideas about why it happened. In the course of exposure to the concepts, activities, and materials they are developing high-level problem-solving strategies that youngsters in bilingual schools rarely experience because everyone is so concerned about their limited English proficiency.

## Achievement Results

Starting in 1979, the Program for Complex Instruction collected achievement data from children experiencing the Finding Out approach and compared their scores in a fall and spring testing (early and late during the curriculum experience) to the gains expected in a nationally normed population.

The children came largely from working-class backgrounds; many of them were attending predominantly Hispanic schools in different districts in the Bay Area of California.

In 1979, 253 students from nine classrooms in San Jose were given the Language Assessment Scales (De Avila & Duncan, 1977) early and late in the year. This is a measure of oral proficiency in English and Spanish that is widely used in the United States. Results showed highly significant gains in oral English proficiency on the part of those children who had started with limited or minimal proficiency in English. The students who gained in language the most dramatically were those who tested with minimal proficiency in *both* English and Spanish (De Avila, 1981). Neves (1983) observed a special set of these children with varying language proficiency and found that the more frequently the Spanish monolingual children were talking about the task, the larger were their gains in the English language. This was true even though these children were largely talking in Spanish, but one must remember that they were functioning in heterogeneous groups where English was being spoken.

In all three years that we have collected data on the Comprehensive Test of Basic Skills (CTBS, 1981), we have found highly significant gains in language arts, reading, and mathematics subtests. In 1983–84, the CTBS science test was employed for the first time, and it too showed significant gains. Comparing these gains to those expected in the normed population revealed that the students were gaining more than the national normed population in every subtest of the battery. Particularly striking were the big gains that occurred each year in such subtests as math concepts and applications, math computation, and reading comprehension.

Just as important as these broad-gauge achievement gains was the research that showed how these gains were connected to specific experiences in the classroom. For example, when we visited the classrooms and systematically counted the number of children who were engaged in talking or in talking and manipulating the materials, we found that the proportion so engaged was very closely related to the gains on the math concepts and applications subtest. In other words, students whose teachers set the stage for more talking and working together had higher average gains on the section of the math test that dealt with concepts and problem solving. Similarly, Stevenson (1982) found that the more children talked and worked together, the better were the inferences they made on their worksheets. Groupwork is the ideal setting for fostering the grasp of abstract concepts.

Where did the gains in language arts come from? A visit to a Finding Out classroom reveals many students who are studying the activity cards and worksheets, arguing about what they say and what they are supposed to be doing. Those classrooms that had a higher proportion of students reading and writing had higher gains in the test of reading comprehension (Cohen & Intili, 1981). Students are reading and writing for a purpose and not in some seatwork exercise that does not make much sense to them.

In one second-grade classroom the teacher told the students every day, "Don't touch the materials until you discuss what the activity card says and can tell me what you are supposed to be doing. I am going to come around and ask one of you to tell me what you are going to do." She would do exactly that, often asking nonreaders what they were planning to do with the materials. If the child could not explain, she would say, "I think you are going to have to read and discuss some more. I'll be back to see if you have figured it out." Navarrete (1985) made videotapes of groups at work in this classroom. She found that much of the discussion among the children centered on figuring out what the activity card said. The more frequently children sought help, received help, and returned to their task (what Navarrete calls a complete problem-solving sequence), the greater were their gains in reading comprehension. Nonreaders were stimulated to find out for themselves what the activity card said because they were anxious to move on to the interesting manipulable materials. In this way the teacher was able to produce gains in basic skills at the same time as her class registered major gains in the understanding of math concepts.

In 1979, the first year that the Finding Out materials were implemented in the Bay Area, we found that some teachers were unable to let go and allow the children to work out things for themselves. Some cut down the number of learning centers in operation so that they and their aides could supervise the resulting fewer groups directly. When teachers failed to delegate authority, there were fewer opportunities for students to talk and work together. In certain classrooms where this failure to delegate authority occurred, there was much less satisfactory implementation and far fewer learning gains than in classrooms where teachers allowed students to solve problems for themselves (Cohen & Intili, 1982). Since 1979, we have found that the introduction of cooperative training and the use of roles is a great help in assisting the teachers to let go. With the children really well trained and with some children helping to keep track of others, teachers feel that the classroom is still under good control even though they are not supervising everyone personally (Cohen & De Avila, 1983).

Although high status children still talk more than low status children in groups at the learning centers, the introduction of cooperative norms, roles, and the discussion of multiple abilities during orientations and wrap-ups has greatly weakened the impact of status on learning gains from what we found in the first year of implementation. Low status children are much more likely to interact as a result of pretraining and thus gain access to the task by receiving assistance. As a result they are learning more than they would have without these special features of cooperative training, roles, and multiple ability treatments.

## CONCLUSION

Because educators have such an overwhelming concern with language acquisition, the curriculum for students with limited English proficiency is often so narrow that it limits the students' intellectual development. In addition, the overwhelming emphasis on language can make both students and teachers self-conscious about language usage. Groupwork is an alternative approach that puts language in a useful perspective; language serves as communication in order to accomplish various learning objectives. For example, in the Finding Out approach, people talk about challenging concepts because they want to understand, to communicate with peers, and to learn how to solve problems. Language is used in a meaningful context. It is used to describe, analyze, hypothesize, and infer. Moreover, insofar as possible, children have access to a language that they can understand.

In classrooms where children ordinarily score around the thirtieth percentile in the fall, the achievement results of using Finding Out are impressive. What can we learn from this experience? Mainly I think we should remember that these results came about as a consequence of carefully designed, theoretically sound learning materials, and as a consequence of hard work on the part of the volunteer teaching teams. Starting in 1982 the implementation was much more consistent from classroom to classroom, and the achievement results were correspondingly stronger. This was a consequence of a two-week training for the teachers, and of a classroom management system using cooperative groups that was very carefully researched and implemented. Finally, these results came about as a result of extensive support for the classroom teachers by school personnel and our staff. Without all this I do not believe that our results for the last three years would be as consistent and powerful as they have been.

What if you have no access to such a high-power approach? You can still put many of the central principles used in Finding Out to work. You can put language into its proper perspective as a tool of communication in a group that is trying to learn something worthwhile. You can use talking and working together to teach concepts. You can implement the Finding Out classroom management system of cooperative norms and roles. You can create classroom learning centers by adapting from recommended activities in texts rich tasks with manipulable materials that illustrate concepts. You can teach children how to help each other across language barriers. You can provide situations that are rich in comprehensible input and opportunities to converse with peers. You can show children how to use each other as resources so that classrooms with students who are behind grade level need not be deprived of grade-level curriculum or of higher level thinking skills.

In fifteen years of work with teachers and with classroom research, I have found nothing so gratifying as the sight of language minority students working excitedly in groups, learning how to solve difficult intellectual problems for themselves. It is my hope that you who teach such students will decide to design a setting where you too can watch young scholars talking and learning together.

# 11 The Multi-Ability Classroom

Treating status problems only with groupwork tasks has its limitations in the classroom setting. The introduction of groupwork tasks without any status treatment will actually activate status problems. Although the use of status treatments makes it possible to produce situations where low status students speak up and participate and where they are considered competent and influential on specific tasks, in most cases these effects will not transfer to other areas of the curriculum. Why not? There are features of conventional classrooms that reconstruct the status order just as fast as you can treat it in the context of groupwork. Conventional classrooms that place an emphasis on drill, recitation, and ability grouping; have a narrow view of curriculum; and rely on marking and grading as the sole method of evaluation, will reinforce beliefs about the intellectual incompetence of low status children.

Sociological analysis and research lead to an alternative model of classroom instruction, the multi-ability classroom, where there are multiple means of achieving success for students and multiple methods of evaluation. The multi-ability classroom means permanent changes in the organization of student work and evaluation practices. These changes are designed to increase active, engaged learning behavior on the part of low status students and to provide enriched detailed feedback to all students on how they are doing on many different and specific skills.

## DEFINITION OF A MULTI-ABILITY CLASSROOM

The multi-ability classroom has many dimensions of intellectual competence. No one student is likely to be rated highly on all these dimensions. Each individual is likely to be rated highly on at least one dimension. Thus, there are no students who are generally expected to be superior regardless of the nature of the task. Basically, the model requires changes in the underlying conception of human ability and changes in the organization of work and evaluation processes in the classroom.

In a multi-ability classroom there are many legitimate intellectual methods of solving problems. For example, students can solve problems visually, spatially, by talking and arguing about solutions, or through imaginative role playing. There are also many different kinds of tasks: discussion, manipulation, visual representation, long-term projects, interaction with community members, dramatization, construction, and experimentation.

In the multi-ability classroom it is legitimate for students to ask each other for help in reading and understanding written materials. It is often the specific duty of one member of the group to see to it that everyone understands the written instructions. However, the capacity to read is only *one* of the many relevant skills that are described by the teacher as important for the learning activity involved.

## THE SINGLE-ABILITY CLASSROOM

The multi-ability classroom can be contrasted with highly conventional classrooms—I will call them single-ability classrooms. Take Ms. Trent's third-grade classroom as an imaginary example. Ms. Trent's day always starts with round-robin reading groups. There are three ability groups, the Lions, the Monkeys, and the Turkeys. She reads with one group while the others work on their language arts kits. These kits have been color coded so that children work on worksheets of a color representing their ability level. The next period is math; Ms. Trent explains how to do fractions to the whole class. She asks certain children to do sample problems at the board and publicly evaluates their performance. Then she assigns word problems using fractions on ditto worksheets to all but eight children (seven of whom are Turkeys). This group is given worksheets reviewing number facts because she feels that they are not yet ready for fractions. After lunch it is time for social studies. The teacher asks all the students to read a chapter of the textbook to themselves. She then talks about the chapter and asks them to write answers to the comprehension questions provided in the text. The day finishes with penmanship and quiet reading time.

Ms. Trent uses quizzes and tests to evaluate students in math and social studies. She marks the wrong answers in red and gives a letter grade or number so that students know how well they did. Outstanding papers are posted on the bulletin board. All the children's names are listed on the bulletin board with gold stars after their names to represent the number of good test performances they have turned in. There is very little time for art and music except in preparation for holidays. Except for taking care of the class hamster and the collection of autumn leaves, there is no science curriculum.

The children are keenly aware of where everyone stands in reading, math, and social studies. They know what the ability-group labels mean. They can easily compare themselves with others on worksheets, test scores, and gold stars. If they have any doubts about the teacher's evaluation of the relative competence of each student, they can listen to her making public evaluations of student performance. The tasks in this classroom typically require the same reading and pencil-and-paper skills, so that those who are poor readers will almost certainly do poorly on most of the subjects. There are few alternative activities in which they can excel.

## EFFECTS OF SINGLE- AND MULTI-ABILITY CLASSROOMS ON STUDENTS

Single-ability classrooms like Ms. Trent's produce strong agreement between the students as to where each one stands on reading ability or on ability in schoolwork. This agreement, in turn, produces a strong status order. It is only when children perceive themselves in a consensual way as widely different in ability that academic status orders can form. Once an academic status order has formed, the status characteristic of reading ability or academic ability has the power to depress the participation and effort of poor readers and those who are seen as having less ability in schoolwork.

Rosenholtz and Wilson (1980) compared two types of classrooms—those where teachers used standardized tasks (as in seatwork), large-group instruction, and competitive evaluation and gave very little autonomy to students in decision making, and those where teachers used more small groups, individualized materials, and less competitive evaluation. In the first set of classrooms, which resembled the single-ability model described above, the students showed strong agreement with each other on a rank order of fellow students on their ability in reading. In the second set of classrooms, the agreement on where each student stood on reading ability was not so marked. In a further analysis of these data, Rosenholtz and Rosenholtz (1981) found that teachers, peers, and individual students perceived a wider range of ability levels in single-ability classrooms. In other words, in these classrooms some children were perceived as highly superior while others were perceived as very inferior.

In review, task structure and evaluation practices help to create status problems in the classroom. By the same token, if you want to weaken the academic status order, you can change those task and evaluation features that help it to form and that reinforce it daily. Figure 11.1 shows that changes in task structure and evaluation practices will produce changes in the status order.

Figure 11.1 also indicates that the creation of a strong status order has effects on students' effort and participation. Low status students who do not try and do not participate have much less active learning time and less time on task. As a result, they achieve less on standardized measures than students who are more engaged with their tasks (Berliner et al., 1978).

## CREATING THE MULTI-ABILITY CLASSROOM

What changes would be necessary if these sociological ideas were to be applied to classroom practice? In order to change

FIGURE 11.1: Classroom Social Structure

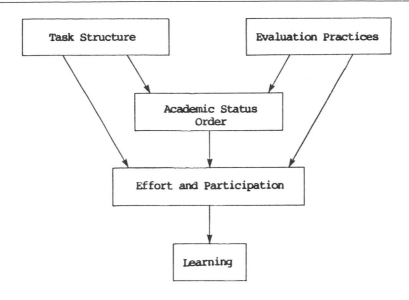

the kinds of human abilities that students see as relevant to classroom success, curricular activities must be closer to the way adults use their minds in the world of work. There must be more stress on problem solving with different acceptable ways to solve problems and different media in which the problem is presented. Classroom activities should include discussion, defending one's point of view, reasoning, logic, experimentation, model building, role playing, spatial and visual problem solving, and conceptual learning.

Psychologists such as Resnick, Glaser, Tyler, and Snow recommend a focus on how the individual brings alternative abilities, aptitudes, or cognitive processes to bear on a particular learning situation. More students will attain intellectual goals if the range of goals is broader; individuals will use multiple intellectual routes to the attainment of goals (Resnick, 1976, p. 9; Tyler, 1976, p. 19; Glaser, 1976, p. 351; Snow, 1978). The purpose of broadening the tasks and teaching objectives is to provide more opportunities for intellectual success and more dimensions on which a student might feel competent.

## Changes in Task Structure

In comparison to a single-ability classroom, a multi-ability classroom has less whole-class instruction, does not use stable ability groups, and uses comparatively little seatwork. Instead there is frequent use of groupwork, multimedia tasks, and students working together at learning centers. These techniques are used when the teaching objective involves conceptual learning. When the goals of learning involve more memorization (such as learning the number facts, spelling, and learning names of places in geography), either traditional drill and recitation or team learning may be employed.

When the teacher finds that certain children need instruction in specific skills, she assembles a temporary group for direct instruction. That group is disbanded when students have mastered the skills. Working with temporary groups presents few management problems because the other students are well trained to take responsibility for their own learning while the teacher is engaged elsewhere. Whole-class instruction clearly has its place in the array of teaching techniques. Teachers may give lively presentations and minilectures to students when orienting them to new topics, new types of learning tasks, or a new set of learning centers. Whole-class discussion is invaluable for interpretation and comprehension of literature, for pulling together what has been learned by various groups, and for dealing with issues of classroom management and general problems of interpersonal process.

Classrooms with such a varied task structure will hinder the formation of a consensual ranking on academic ability, as shown by the model pictured in Figure 11.1. Tasks that are varied do not allow students to make simple unidimensional comparisons with each other. If tasks are carefully defined as requiring multiple abilities, different children will have a chance to excel at different tasks. This will allow low status children to develop some favorable expectations for intellectual competence.

The purpose of the expanded use of groupwork is to improve the participation of all students and to increase in particular the effort, engagement, and participation of the low status or low-achieving student. The use of small groups is associated with higher levels of student engagement as well as academic participation. This connection has been demonstrated in previous classroom research (Hess & Takanishi, 1974; Berliner et al., 1978).

## Task Structure Changes in Integrated Classrooms

In working with a racially integrated and academically heterogeneous intermediate school, the Stanford Status Equalization Project tried to help six teachers change their task structure by introducing more multiple ability tasks and small groups as part of their regular curriculum. The staff held a series of discussions with each classroom teacher on how their regular curriculum might be adapted to the multi-ability model. During three months of in-service work, the staff assisted the teachers with preparing the students for groupwork using discussion skills.

One month later Ahmadjian (1980) carried out a special study in three of the classrooms that had worked with Stanford staff and three classrooms that had not participated in the program. The first three teachers employed small groups frequently, while the second set of teachers made very little use of small groups, relying on large groups and individual seatwork. Ahmadjian repeatedly observed 36 low-achieving students from these six classrooms as they worked in different subject areas of the curriculum, such as social studies and math, that ordinarily require reading.

When the observations were classified as to the kind of grouping and activity in which the student was seen, it was clear that students in the small groups were more likely to be talking about their work with other students than were students in other grouping patterns. In small groups students talked on an average of 1.5 times a minute, while in large groups the rate was .29 interactions per minute; in individual work the rate was .45 interactions per minute. If the students were working in a small group on creative writing, multimedia tasks, role playing, or part of open discussion, the probability of talking about the task rose to an average of 2.5 times a minute. As in Berliner's (1978) study, Ahmadjian found relatively high rates of disengagement in seatwork—50 percent of the time these low-achieving students were scored as "off task."

Small groups were comparatively rare in the classrooms that did not receive in-service training. However, when small groups were observed in these classrooms, they also produced higher rates of talking and engagement, just as they did in the trained classrooms.

## Changes in Evaluation

The multi-ability classroom avoids reliance on competitive marking and grading for evaluation of students as the *only* method of evaluation. Competitive evaluation, in particular, will aggravate status problems; it has the effect of making low status students less willing to participate and to risk receiving a negative evaluation (Awang Had, 1972). This is not to say that students should not know exactly where they stand on objective grounds. On the contrary, evaluation should include some specific feedback to individuals on what they have done well and on what they need to improve. Talking to students specifically about their performance can be combined with conventional marking and grading so that individuals are well aware of their strengths and weaknesses on multiple dimensions.

In a sample of integrated classrooms the Stanford Status Equalization Project found that teachers quite frequently combined traditional marking and grading with a more individualized approach to evaluation in which they talked with individuals specifically about what they did well and where they needed to improve. When this combination occurs, there are several favorable consequences: Children are more likely to believe that they are personally responsible for what marks they get (Oren, 1980)—that is, they are less likely to report that their grades are due to luck or to teacher bias—and minority children who are poor achievers are more likely to think that they have some academic abilities (Macias-Sanchez, 1982).

## Changing Student Perceptions of Abilities

Changing the perception of low-achieving students that they are generally incompetent in school is probably the most difficult task for the classroom teacher. In my work with low status students I have found that they are typically highly resistant to believing that they are intellectually competent even when it is clear to others that they are behaving in a competent fashion.

Strangely enough, I have found it somewhat easier to improve their learning outcomes than to alter the tendency of everyone to perceive them as less competent in small-group interaction. The introduction of well-designed groupwork will have the effect of improving their engagement, participation, and learning outcomes. Beyond this strategy, one must still be concerned with what is happening within small work groups. In the *Finding Out/Descubrimiento* classrooms, it was still the case that high status children participated more frequently than low status children. Similarly, it was easier for the Status Equalization Project to produce harmonious interracial discussion groups in desegregated settings than it was to change the perception that poor readers do not make intellectually important contributions (Cohen, 1982; Gamero, 1981). Unless expectations for competence are fundamentally changed, low status students will continue to be less active and influential within the small work groups.

You can attack this problem while groups are working on rich tasks defined as requiring multiple abilities. Take the time to observe low status students while they are working in a group so that you can see them exhibiting reasoning behavior, visual or spatial skills, or precision in thinking, drawing, or manipulation—or making any intellectual contribution to the group. Immediately tell the student specifically and publicly what fine work he or she is doing. Be sure to make clear exactly what the student has done well.

This is one of the most powerful strategies a teacher can use because it takes advantage of his or her great power to confer evaluations on students that they will believe. This maneuver should not be confused with reinforcing unsuccessful students even when they have made mistakes or have made a contribution that is not helpful for the group, a practice that will have destructive effects on the student's sense of competence and should always be avoided.

## A FRESH LOOK AT INSTRUCTION

The discussion has implied certain general criteria for looking at tasks and evaluation practices. In examining the kinds of tasks you select for instruction, ask yourself the following questions: What opportunities do low achievers have for success in my classroom? Do classroom tasks and objectives provide multiple dimensions of competence? Is reading a prerequisite for successful participation on all important tasks? How often do I use multimedia tasks and small groups?

Also give consideration to your evaluation practices. Some of the questions you might ask yourself are: What are the ways that I provide for students to evaluate their own competence and the competence of others? Do I use ability grouping with more or less stable membership? Are competitive marks and grades the only basis the children have for knowing how well they are succeeding? If the low-achieving students do succeed, do their classmates have a chance to see and evaluate that success? Do the low-achieving students know clearly what they have done that is successful and what needs to be improved?

If you are dissatisfied with the answers to these questions for your classroom, you may wonder where to start making changes. The best way to start is to find a like-minded colleague with whom you can work. Develop some multiple ability tasks, carry them out, and evaluate them. Pay careful attention to what happens to low status students within their groups. When they display competent behavior, try to provide some specific and public feedback for them.

Once you have mastered these skills, you have already completed the hardest part of the recommended changes. You will then be ready to enrich activities designed to meet curricular requirements. Integrating many of the basic skills within more challenging groupwork tasks as described in the previous chapter is the key to finding time to meet multiple objectives set for your grade level. Science and social studies are prime candidates for meeting such multiple objectives with groupwork techniques.

At the high school level, the pressures for evaluation are intense. Conventional examinations are quite consistent with the multi-ability classroom, as long as all your students have had equal access to the learning required for those examinations and have not been shut out by reading comprehension problems, by the unavailability of peer assistance in preparation for the exam, or by the narrow way in which the materials were presented. Finding time to talk systematically to individual students is not an easy task for a high school teacher working with 35 students in a 50-minute period. Although all students benefit from this kind of talk, it is the less successful student who is in the most critical need of feedback.

The multi-ability classroom should produce desirable effects on students you have regarded as the hardest to reach. They will put out more effort, spend more time on task, and approach assignments and tests with a more positive attitude and increased expectations for competence. Most of the teachers I have worked with earnestly wish to be effective with less successful students. In the final analysis, it is the joy of seeing these students begin to achieve that motivates many of us to continue the difficult process of changing the work of the classroom.

# Appendixes
# Bibliography
# Index

# APPENDIX A

# Cooperative Training Exercises

## Making Students Sensitive to Needs of Others in a Group

### BROKEN CIRCLES

The instructions to the participants and suggested discussion given below are those of the developers of Broken Circles, Nancy and Ted Graves (Graves & Graves, 1985), who also sell laminated sets of the broken circles (see note in reference entry). Broken Circles is based on the Broken Squares game invented by Dr. Alex Bavelas (1973).

The class is divided into groups of 3–6 persons. Each person is given an envelope with different pieces of the circle. The goal is for each person to put together a complete circle. In order for this goal to be reached, there must be some exchange of pieces. Players are not allowed to talk or to take pieces from someone else's envelope. They may only give.

### Instructions to the participants

Each of you will be given an envelope containing two or three pieces of a puzzle, but don't open it until I say so. The object of this game is to put these pieces together in such a way that each member of your group ends up with a complete circle. There are a few rules to make the game more fun.

1. This game must be played in complete silence. No talking.

2. You may not point or signal to other players with your hands in any way.
3. Each player must put together his or her own circle. No one else may show a player how to do it or do it for him or her.
4. This is a giving game. You may not take a piece from another player, but you may *give* your pieces, one at a time, to any other member of your group, and other group members may give pieces to you. You may not place a piece in another person's puzzle; players must complete only their own puzzles. Instead, hand the piece to the other player, or place it beside the other pieces in front of him or her.

Now you may take the pieces out of your envelope and place them in front of you, colored side up. This is a group task, and you will have 15–20 minutes to make your circles.

Remember, the game is not finished until each of you at your table has completed a circle. When all of you have finished, raise your hands. (If one group finishes before the others, suggest that they try to discover if there are any *other* ways they could put the pieces together to form different circles.)

### Discussion

When all groups have completed the task or the allotted time has ended, the teacher should help the participants to identify some of the important things that happened, analyze why they happened, and generalize to other group learning situations. The following questions can serve as a guide to the discussion:

What do you think this game was all about?
How do you feel about what happened in your group today?
What things did you do in your group that helped you to be successful in solving the problem?
What things did you do that made it harder?
What could the groups do better in the future?

Help participants to be concrete about what they did and also abstract about the general implications of what they did and the lessons they learned for the future.

Directions for making and using Broken Circles are given below. If there is time, or if the teacher feels the lesson is useful, it is possible to play a variation called Advanced Broken Circles, and directions for this game are also provided. The difference is that in

Advanced Broken Circles, one player may block the task for the rest of the group by completing his or her circle satisfactorily but refusing to share some pieces with the others. This second task can always be done later in the year if the teacher feels that this particular lesson needs to be discussed.

### Patterns to use for different age children

*Simplest Broken Circles.*   This pattern is suitable for children 5–7 years old in groups of three. Sort the pieces into three envelopes (I, II, and III, as marked in Figure A.1) and give one envelope to each player. Figure A.1 indicates one solution; in this solution each player must give up some of his or her pieces to other players. The diagram shows how pieces held by players I, II, and III can be rearranged to form three circles. Two circles composed of a half and two quarters represents an alternative solution.

*Simple Broken Circles.*   This pattern is suitable for children 8–10 years old in groups of four. Sort the pieces into four envelopes marked W, X, Y, and Z. The diagram at the top of Figure A.2 indicates one solution. Ask the groups that finish first, "How many *other* ways of forming four circles can you discover?" Alternative solutions are pictured at the bottom of Figure A.2.

*Advanced Broken Circles.*   This pattern is suitable for children 8–10 years old who have had some experience with Simple Broken Circles. It may also be used as a first exercise with older children, high school students, and adults.

### Instructions for making a set of broken circles
Make your sets (one per group) from heavy cardboard, with the circles about 20 cm in diameter. Each set of six circles should be a

FIGURE A.1: Simplest Broken Circles

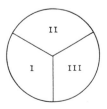 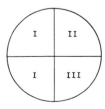 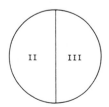

FIGURE A.2: Simple Broken Circles

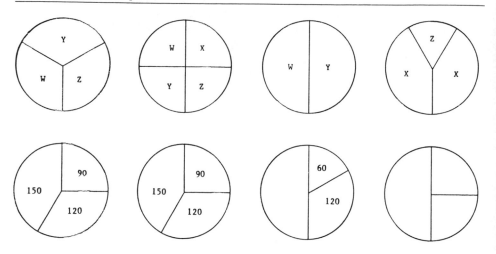

FIGURE A.3: Advanced Broken Circles

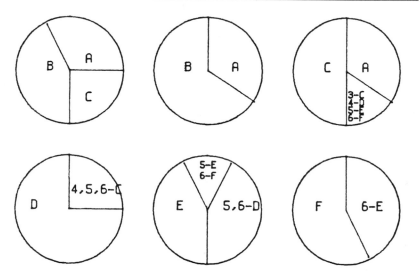

different color, with the letters and numbers (indicating which pieces go into which envelopes for groups of different sizes) marked on the back of each piece. Angles used are 60°, 90°, 120°, 150°, 180°, 210°, 240°, and 270°.

In Figure A.3 the numbers indicate the group size; the letters indicate the proper envelope. If a piece has no number on it, it remains in its lettered envelope regardless of group size.

Take all the pieces with only a letter on them and put them into envelopes marked with those letters. These never change. The placement of the other four pieces varies with the size of the group. For example, if you are playing with six-person groups, then the piece marked 6-F (60°) goes into the F envelope, the 6-E piece (150°) into the E envelope, the 6-C piece (90°) into the C envelope, and the 6-D piece (150°) into the D envelope. Repeat this pattern for each six-person group.

Although it is fairly easy on the spot to modify a set of six circles for groups of five or less, once you are familiar with the exercise, it is easier to make up and label sets of varying sizes in advance. Then these can be quickly substituted when required.

### JIGSAW PUZZLES

Pick out some simple jigsaw puzzles. Each group member has a bag with one quarter of the pieces (for a four-person group). They have to complete the puzzle without a picture of the product in front of them. They may talk, but the task cannot be completed without each individual contributing his or her share. One child may not take another's piece and do it for him or her. Hints and encouragement may be given, but all the members must do their own part.

Following this exercise, hold a discussion similar to that suggested for Broken Circles. Bring out how this will be useful during groupwork. Students will each have information and ideas that will help complete the tasks given to the groups. By sharing this information and these insights with others, everyone will be able to benefit by learning more from the activity.

## Preparing Elementary Students for Learning Centers with Individual Worksheets and Manipulable Materials

In order to work in this setting students will have to learn how to help and explain, to ask questions, and to give good answers. We suggest two exercises, Master Designer and Guess My Rule, for teaching new behaviors concerning helping and explaining. You may wish to develop your own using these as examples of how to pick out a situation that highlights and gives practice to new behaviors.

## MASTER DESIGNER

### Materials

This game requires a set of geometric shapes. Each player needs a complete set, but one person in each group takes the role of observer and does not require a set. A total of five persons per group is recommended, but smaller groups are acceptable. The shapes should be made out of some sturdy material such as oaktag. The exact size of these shapes is given in Figure A.4.

In addition, you will need some cardboard or other dividers that can be stood on a table. The idea is that each player can see the other members of the group over the divider but *cannot* see what the others are doing with their pieces.

### Rules and Discussion

One person plays the role of the master designer. This person has to instruct the other players as to how to replicate a design he or she has created with the pieces (all or part of them), but the master designer cannot do this task for them. Players cannot see what the others are doing, nor can they see the design of the master. However, group members may ask questions of the master designer. This illustrates an important new behavior:

Helping students do things for themselves

The group is dependent on the master designer for explaining how it should be done. This is the second new behavior:

Explain by telling how

FIGURE A.4: "Master Designer" Shapes

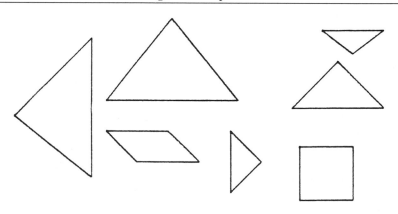

In addition to verbal directions, children may use sign language to demonstrate to each other. This will help bridge any language differences you may have in your class.

When any member of the group feels that he or she has figured out the master design, the designer is asked to check the solution. If the master designer says it is correct, then that player too is to help others in the group by explaining how. This rule illustrates another important new behavior:

Everybody helps

Make up a bright chart with these three behaviors and display it prominently in the classroom.

After everyone in the group has completed the correct design, another student can take the role of the master designer. If you do not have time for everyone to take a turn, pick a variety of children to play this role—not just the natural leaders.

One student plays the role of observer for each round. The observer watches the group and checks off every time he or she sees two of the three new behaviors occur. These are

Explain by telling how
Everybody helps

Also make up a simple scoring sheet so the observer can check off new behaviors every time he or she sees them.

Since this is the first time students have ever been asked to observe, you will need to discuss how a person would know that a student is "telling how" or whether or not other members than the master designer are helping. You might want to run through a simple design first with yourself as master designer. Then have students role-play "telling how" and "helping others." It is not so important that the observer correctly record every time the behavior happens. The fact that someone is watching for and checking off behaviors helps to objectify behavior and will assist the whole group in recognizing such behaviors when they occur.

After the game ask each observer to report how many times he or she saw each new behavior. The observer may be able to give some good examples of what was seen. This provides an opportunity for the teacher to reinforce the new behaviors. Follow this with a discussion similar to the one described in detail for Broken Circles. Discuss how these behaviors will be useful for the curriculum. Explain that everyone will have to do his or her own worksheet, so it will be important that everyone comes to understand and do things for themselves.

GUESS MY RULE

### Objective

This is a game that Rosenholtz (1977) developed to illustrate reasoning skills. Students must deduce a central principle which accounts for all the different colored sizes and shapes that may be placed in the center of a ring. Someone holds a card, called a Rule Card, on which the central principle, such as "Only red shapes," is written. The rule card holder tells the players whether or not their choice of a playing card fits the rule or not.

### Materials

Each group of five (three players, one rule card holder, and one observer) will need to have a set of rule cards, a large circle of yarn, and a special deck of playing cards. Each playing card displays one of four different shapes (circle, square, triangle, and diamond) in one of three sizes (large, medium, and small) and one of three colors (red, blue, and green); making up one card for each possible combination of shape, size, and color results in a deck of 36 cards. Outline the particular shape in the right size and color on the front of each card, and repeat the color on the border of the card. (It is much easier to draw the shapes on uniform card stock than it is to cut out cards in each shape, and the deck made with uniform cards is also much easier for the children to manipulate.) For each group of players you will also need to make up a set of rule cards. These are the cards with the central principle that the players must deduce. The rules are provided in Figure A.5.

### Instructions to students

This reasoning game is called "Guess My Rule" and is played with this special deck of cards. As you can see, there are four different shapes in the deck: a circle, a square, a triangle, and a diamond. Each shape comes in three sizes: big, medium, and small. And each size in each shape comes in three different colors: red, blue, and green. There are many ways to sort these cards into categories. I want you each to think of a way. Here I have some rule cards that have on them

FIGURE A.5: Rule Cards for "Guess My Rule"

1)     Only △  s

2)     Only smallest shapes

3)     Only BIGGEST ◇  s

4)     Only red* shapes

5)     Only blue* ▭  s

6)     Only red* and blue* ○  s

*Outline these colors and shapes
in the appropriate colors.

different ways to sort the deck into various categories. The object of "Guess My Rule" is for you to try to reason out which rule card I am holding. We will put the playing cards in the center of the table, and you will each take turns picking one card. If the card you've picked fits my rule, I will say "yes," and you can put it in the yarn circle. If the card you've picked doesn't fit my rule, I will say "no," and you can put it outside the yarn circle. Each person can only pick one card at each turn. Once you've found a couple of cards that fit the rule you can try to reason out what my rule is, but you can only try to guess my rule when it is your turn to pick a card.

(The teacher takes one group and plays one simple round with the teacher as rule card holder. The other children gather round to watch.)

As you can see this is a game that requires reasoning and some very careful thinking. Many of the things you will be doing at the learning centers will require reasoning and thinking. When people have such a difficult problem to solve, one thing they can do is *find out what others think.*

We are going to practice finding out what others think. When it is your turn and you have an idea what the rule is, ask the two other players in your group what they think about your idea. You might say, "I think the rule is all blue shapes. Do you think that's the rule?" If they say yes or no, ask them to *tell why* they think that. After you listen to what they say or if they don't know, ask the other person the same questions. Then *make up your own mind* about what you think is the rule and ask the rule card holder.

### Discussion

Have the children practice asking each other what they think and why they think so. Discuss with them why it is important to try and tell why. This is an important new skill.

A third rule is also important preparation for working at learning centers. Because each student is responsible for his or her own worksheet, it is important that all the students feel responsible for making their own decisions about what to do after consulting others.

All these new behaviors ("Find out what others think," "Tell why," and "Make your own decision") should be printed on a chart and prominently displayed.

As in the previous game there should be an observer. The two behaviors an observer can hear and see are

Finding out what others think.
Telling why.

The person who is the observer should have a simple check sheet parallel to the one for Master Designer, but with the new behaviors on it.

You are now ready to have each group play the game and take turns with the various roles. One person is the rule card holder, one is the observer, and the other three are players. After each round, other group members get to be rule card holder and observer. The new rule card holder picks up a new card from the deck, which is face down.

After the game, have the observers report how many times they saw the new behaviors on the round they scored. Ask the children to discuss whether or not it was helpful to them to get other people's opinions. See if you can pick up some good examples of children's telling "why" if they don't come up with these themselves. Have them comment on what it is like to hear opinions different than one's own and to have to consider those ideas before making up one's own mind. Ask them if they know of any other situation that is like this. Point out that they will have to do this at the learning centers.

## Preparing Students for Groupwork That Features Group Discussion

### EPSTEIN'S FOUR-STAGE ROCKET

This is the original task designed by Epstein (1972) to improve discussion skills of any age group. There are some minor adaptations of the original version in the material presented.

### Pretest

Explain to the class that in order to prepare for the groupwork, they need to learn what it takes to have a good group discussion. Divide the class into five-person groups. Give the groups a highly interesting task to discuss. (Two sample discussion tasks are given at the end of Appendix A.) The teacher circulates, listening, observing, and taking notes on examples of good and bad discussion technique. The groups are allowed to discuss for five minutes.

### Practicing the four stages

After the pretest, hold a group discussion on what makes for good discussion and what the barriers are. Tell the class that they are going to practice four skills that are necessary so that a discussion can take off like a rocket (use an illustration of a rocket with four stages) by following the instructions given below.

*Stage I, Conciseness*—"getting quickly to the point and not beating around the bush."

> Select a timekeeper who will watch the clock and keep time for the group. Keep on discussing the subject for five minutes. The timekeeper makes sure that *each person talks for only fifteen seconds*.

*Stage II, Listening*—"paying attention to what is being said."

> Select a new timekeeper. Keep on discussing the same subject for five more minutes, again making sure that each person talks for only fifteen seconds. This time, however, *each person must wait three seconds after the person before has spoken before he or she may speak*.

*Stage III, Reflecting*—"repeating out loud to the group something of what the person before you has said."

> Select a new timekeeper. Keep on discussing the same subject, making sure that each person talks for only fifteen seconds and that he waits three seconds after the person before has spoken before he or she speaks. In addition, *everyone who speaks must begin by repeating to the group something that was said by the person who*

*spoke immediately before*. This is called *reflecting*. The person who had spoken before has to nod his or her head to mean yes if he or she thinks this reflection is right. The new speaker may not continue until he or she correctly reflects what the person before has said.

*Stage IV, Everyone contributes*—"all the people in the group have to speak."

Select a new timekeeper. Keep on discussing the same subject for five more minutes. All previous rules apply, as well as a new one: *No one may speak a second time until everyone in the group has spoken.*

After each stage ask each timekeeper to report on how well their group did on the skill being practiced. The timekeeper may have other observations to make about how difficult it was and what happened. Remind the class why each skill is important.

### Posttest

Select a person as observer who has not yet had a chance to play a role like timekeeper. Hold five more minutes of discussion without having to observe the rules but trying to use the skills of *conciseness, listening, reflecting,* and *contributions by everyone*. Observers will note down every time they see good examples of each of these behaviors. You may want to create a scoring sheet.

After the posttest, ask observers to tell what they observed. Also ask the whole class what were some of the differences between the pretest and the posttest.

*Note:* Unless the class has had some previous experience with discussion, you will find that they will finish discussion tasks very rapidly. You will need to have alternative questions or tasks prepared. Sample discussion tasks are given at the end of this Appendix.

### IMPROVING GROUP PROCESS SKILLS

The Four-Stage-Rocket may be enough to get the groupwork started. However, there are additional skills, especially for group projects, that become more important as groups attempt longer-term, more ambitious projects. Elizabeth Hunter (1972) has developed lists of helping and troublesome behaviors for improving group process skills; the lists that follow are adapted from Hunter's work.

*Work behaviors* are ways that help to get the group's work done. A skillful group member

Has *new ideas* or suggestions
Asks for or gives information
Helps to explain better
Pulls ideas together
Finds out if the group is ready to decide what to do

*Helping behaviors* are ways that help the group keep working smoothly all together. A helpful group member

Gets people together
Brings other people in
Shows interest and kindness
Is willing to change own ideas if someone makes a good argument
Tells others in a good way how they are behaving

*Troublesome behaviors* are problems that come up between people in the group and stop them from getting their work done. A troublesome group member

Attacks other people
Won't go along with other people's suggestions
Talks too much
Keeps people from discussing because he or she does not like arguments
Shows that he or she does not care about what is happening
Lets someone boss the group
Does not talk and contribute ideas
Tells stories and keeps the group from getting their work done

*Choose a small number of these behaviors that you think are of critical importance based on what you think the group will need or problems that you have observed during discussions.* It is always better if the class members can select behaviors that need work on the basis of their own experience. Explain to the class that this exercise will help them with these particular skills.

Divide the class into discussion groups after you have presented to them the set of behaviors they are going to be working on. Always use the same label to refer to the selected behaviors. Select one observer for each group who will write down every time one of these particular behaviors occurs. Draw up a scoring sheet. Take observers aside in advance and make sure they know how to observe these particular behaviors. Give the groups a discussion topic that they can work on for five or ten minutes.

Stop the discussion and ask observers to report what they have seen and scored. Pull out from the discussion some good strategies that have been used or alternative strategies to deal with problems that have arisen. The same basic format can be used for any number of skills that you think require practice.

## Sample Discussion Tasks

### SPACE SHIP

The object of this game is to select seven persons to go into a space ship for a voyage to a new planet. You have just been alerted that a neutron bomb is headed for the United States and the United States has just released a neutron bomb in retaliation. Therefore, it is very likely the end of the world. The space ship has the capacity to set up life on a new planet. Eleven persons have been chosen by lot to go on the ship; however, an error was made, and now it turns out that there is only room for seven. Your group must decide which seven persons will go to start life on the new planet. Remember, only seven persons can fit in the ship. You must have an agreement of the entire group before a selection can be made.

1. A 30-year-old male symphony orchestra violin player
2. A 67-year-old male minister
3. A 23-year-old engineer and his 21-year-old wife (they refuse to be separated)
4. A 40-year-old policeman who refuses to be separated from his gun
5. A male student of your own age from your school
6. A 25-year-old male high school dropout, recently arrested for armed robbery
7. A 32-year-old female sixth-grade teacher
8. A 40-year-old female doctor (medical)
9. A 50-year-old female artist and sculptor
10. A 25-year-old male poet
11. A 1-year-old female child

## ALLIGATOR RIVER

Once there was a girl named Abigail who was in love with a boy named Gregory. Gregory had an unfortunate accident and broke his glasses. Abigail, being a true friend, volunteered to take them to be repaired. But the repair shop was across the river, and during a flash flood the bridge was washed away. Poor Gregory could see nothing without his glasses, so Abigail was desperate to get across the river to the repair shop. While she was standing forlornly on the bank of the river, clutching the broken glasses in her hands, a boy named Sinbad glided by in a rowboat.

She asked Sinbad if he would take her across. He agreed to on the condition that while she was having the glasses repaired, she would go to a nearby store and steal a transistor radio that he had been wanting. Abigail refused to do this and went to see a friend named Ivan who had a boat.

When Abigail told Ivan her problem, he said he was too busy to help her out and didn't want to be involved. Abigail, feeling that she had no other choice, returned to Sinbad and told him she would agree to his plan.

When Abigail returned the repaired glasses to Gregory, she told him what she had had to do. Gregory was so mad at what she had done he told her that he never wanted to see her again.

Abigail, upset, turned to Slug with her tale of woe. Slug was so sorry for Abigail that he promised her he would get even with Gregory. They went to the school playground where Gregory was playing ball and Abigail watched happily while Slug beat Gregory up and broke his glasses.

*Rank these characters from "best" to "worst":* Abigail, Gregory, Sinbad, Ivan, Slug. *Give reasons for your decisions.* (Simon, Howe, & Kirschenbaum, 1972, pp. 292–93)

# APPENDIX B

# Tools for Groupwork Evaluation

## SAMPLE STUDENT QUESTIONNAIRE

Name: _____

Please mark with an "X" on the line to the left of each answer that is most like how you feel for each question. Remember, this is not a test. There are no right answers. I want to know what you think.

### Section A

1. How interesting did you find your work in the group?
   _____ a. Very Interesting.
   _____ b. Fairly Interesting.
   _____ c. Somewhat interesting.
   _____ d. Not very Interesting.
   _____ e. I was not interested at all.
2. How difficult did you find your work in the group?
   _____ a. Extremely difficult
   _____ b. Fairly difficult
   _____ c. Sometimes difficult
   _____ d. Not too difficult—just about right
   _____ e. Very easy
3. Did you understand exactly what the group was supposed to do?
   _____ a. I knew just what to do.
   _____ b. At first I didn't understand.
   _____ c. It was never clear to me.
4. *For Multiple Ability Tasks*
   a. What abilities did you think were important for doing a good job on this task?

     b. Was there one ability on which you thought you did very well?
        _____Yes   _____No

5. How many times did you have the chance to talk during the group sessions today?
     _____ a. None
     _____ b. One or two times
     _____ c. Three to four times
     _____ d. Five or more times

6. If you talked less than you wanted to, what were the main reasons?
     _____ a. I felt afraid to give my opinion.
     _____ b. Somebody else interrupted me.
     _____ c. I was not given the chance to give my opinion.
     _____ d. I talked as much as I wanted to.
     _____ e. Nobody paid attention to what I said.
     _____ f. I was not interested in the problem.
     _____ g. I was not feeling well today.

7. Did you get along with everybody in your group?
     _____ a. With few of them
     _____ b. With half of them
     _____ c. With most of them
     _____ d. With all of them
     _____ e. With none of them

8. How many students listened to each other's ideas?
     _____ a. Only a few of them
     _____ b. Half of them
     _____ c. Most of them
     _____ d. All of them, except one
     _____ e. All of them

## Section B

1. Who did the most talking in your group today?
2. Who did the least talking in your group today?
3. Who had the best ideas in your group today?
4. Who did most to direct the discussion?
5. Would you like to work with this group again?
     _____Yes   _____No
     If not, why not?
6. How well do you think the facilitator did today in his or her job?

## GUIDE TO ANALYZING THE STUDENT QUESTIONNAIRE

I. What percentage of the class found the task uninteresting, too difficult, or confusing? (Questions A, B, and C below will show you how to calculate the answer using student responses to Section A, questions 1–3.)

   A. What percentage of the students reported that the work was not very interesting or they were not interested at all? (Add up the number of students who chose c or d on question 1. Divide this number by total who turned in questionnaires to obtain a percentage.)

   B. What percentage of the students reported that the work was extremely difficult or very easy? (Add up the number of students who chose a or e on question 2. Use the same procedure as above to obtain a percentage.)

   C. What percentage of the students reported that the instructions were never clear to them? (Determine the number of students who chose c in question 3. Follow the same procedure as above to obtain a percentage.)

II. *For multiple ability tasks:* Did the students see the task as involving multiple abilities? (Use Section A of the student questionnaire.)

   A. How many students were able to list more than one ability? (Question 4a)

   B. How many students were able to list one ability on which they thought they did well? (Question 4b)

   C. How many of the abilities listed were like those in ordinary schoolwork? (Question 4b)

III. How was the group process? Are there special problems that need further work?

   A. What kinds of problems are checked off frequently on Section A, question 6?

   B. How many students report getting along with half or fewer members of their group? (Section A, question 7; add up a, b, and e.)

   C. How many students report that half or fewer members of their group listened? (Section A, question 8; add up a and b.)

IV. How did the low status students feel about their experience? (Pull out their questionnaires and make tabulations listed below.)

   A. How many of these students found the task uninteresting, too difficult, or confusing? How does this number compare to the total number of students in the class who felt this way? *If a much higher percentage of low status students were unhappy with the task than the overall percentage for the class calculated in Section I, then your task was particularly unsuccessful with low status students.*

B. *For Multiple Ability Tasks:* How many of the low status students reported that there was an ability on which they thought they did well? (Section A, question 4b.) *If the multiple ability treatment is successful, practically all these students should answer yes.*

C. Were these students more likely to report that they rarely participated than the rest of the class? (Count up how many of the low status students chose a or b on question 5 in Section A. Now do the same for the rest of the class.) *If more than half of the low status students reported poor participation, while only 25 percent or fewer of the students in the rest of the class said they participated rarely, then you still have a status problem in participation.*

D. Were there some particular low status students for whom this experience was not a good one? Take those low status students who report little participation on question 5 and examine their questionnaire as a whole to see if you can find out what the source of the trouble was.

V. How successful was each group in achieving equal status and good group process? (Rearrange the questionnaires so you have all the ones from each group together.)

A. Did some groups report more interpersonal problems than others? Or were complaints pretty well spread across groups? (Section A, questions 6, 7, and 8.) If three or more members of the same group make one of these complaints about their experience, one could reasonably infer that this particular group had interpersonal difficulty.

B. Were there any groups in which the low status student was chosen by at least two others as having had the best ideas? This would indicate that you have been successful in treating the status problem in at least some of your groups.

C. In how many groups did almost everyone choose one of the low status students as having done the least talking? (Section B, question 2.) This is a group where you have not achieved equal status behavior. Check the group's questionnaires over

carefully. You may want to appoint this student as facilitator
next time.

D. How were the evaluations of the facilitator in each group
(Section B, question 6)?

E. If the low status student was a facilitator, was he or she chosen by at least some group members as having done the most
to direct the discussion? (Section B, question 4.)

VI. How good were the relations between students of different racial or ethnic or language groups? (Divide the questionnaires by
racial, ethnic, or linguistic group membership.)

A. Did most of the minority students report getting along with
most or all of the other students in their group? (Section A,
question 7.)

B. What proportion of minority vs. majority group said they
would not like to work with their group again? (Section B,
question 5.) Ideally, the proportion should not be much above
15 percent in either category, and it is certainly not a good
sign if the proportion is much higher among minorities than
among majority students.

# References

Aaronson, E. *The jigsaw classroom*. Beverly Hills, Calif.: Sage Publications, 1978.

Ahmadjian, J. *Academic status and reading achievement: Modifying the effects of the self-fulfilling prophecy*. Unpublished doctoral dissertation, Stanford University, 1980.

Anderson, L. M. *Student responses to seatwork: Implications for the study of students' cognitive processing*. Research Series No. 102. East Lansing: Michigan State University, Institute for Research on Teaching, 1982.

Arias, M. B. Teacher and student behaviors in contrasting bilingual settings. Paper presented at the American Educational Research Association meeting, Montreal, 1983.

Awang Had, B. S. *Effects of status and task outcome structures upon observable power and prestige order of small task-oriented groups*. Unpublished doctoral dissertation, Stanford University, 1972.

Bandura, A. *Principles of behavior modification*. New York: Holt, Rinehart & Winston, 1969.

Bavelas, A. The five squares problem—an instructional aid in group cooperation. *Studies in Personnel Psychology*, 1973, *5*, 29–38.

Berger, J., Conner, T., & McKeown, W. Evaluations and the formation and maintenance of performance expectations. In J. Berger, T. Conner, & H. Fisek (Eds.), *Expectation states theory: A theoretical research program*. Cambridge, Mass.: Winthrop Publications, 1974.

Berger, J., Rosenholtz, S. J., & Zelditch, M. Z., Jr. Status organizing processes. *Annual Review of Sociology*, 1980, *6*, 479–508.

Berliner, D., Fisher, C., Filby, N., Marliave, R., Cahen, L., Dishaw, M., & Moore, J. *Beginning teacher evaluation study—teaching behaviors, academic learning time and student achievement: Final report of phase II-B*. San Francisco, Calif.: Far West Laboratory, 1978.

Bloom, J. R., & Schuncke, G. S. The effect of a cooperative curriculum experience on choice of task organization. *Journal of Experimental Education*, 1979, *48*, 84–90.

Breer, P. E., & Locke, E. A. *Task experience as a source of attitudes*. Homewood, Ill.: Dorsey Press, 1965.

Cazden, C. B. *Curriculum language contexts for bilingual education: Language development in a bilingual society*. Los Angeles, Calif.: National Dissemination and Assessment Center, 1979.

Cohen, E. G. Interracial interaction disability. *Human Relations*, 1972, *25*, 9–24.

Cohen, E. G. Expectation states and interracial interaction in school settings. *Annual Review of Sociology*, 1982, *8*, 209–35.

Cohen, E. G. Talking and working together: Status, interaction and learning. In P. Peterson, L. C. Wilkinson, & M. Hallinan (Eds.), *The social context of instruction: Group organization and group processes*. New York: Academic Press, 1984.

Cohen, E. G., & De Avila, E. *Learning to think in math and science: Improving local education for minority children. A final report to the Walter S. Johnson Foundation*. Stanford, Calif.: Stanford University, Program for Complex Instruction, December 1983.

Cohen, E. G., & Intili, J. K. *Interdependence and management in bilingual classrooms: Final report* I (NIE Contract #NIE-G-80-0217). Stanford, Calif.: Center for Educational Research at Stanford, 1981.

Cohen, E. G., & Intili, J. K. *Interdependence and management in bilingual classrooms. Final report* II (NIE Contract #NIE-G-80-0217). Stanford, Calif.: Center for Educational Research at Stanford, 1982.

Cohen, E. G., Intili, J. K., & Robbins, S. Task and authority: A sociological view of classroom management. In D. Duke (Ed.), *The national society for the study of education: 78th Yearbook*. 1979, Part II, 116–43.

Cohen, E. G., Lockheed, M., & Lohman, M. Center for interracial cooperation: A field experiment. *Sociology of Education*, 1976, *49*, 47–58.

Cohen, E. G., & Roper, S. Modification of interracial interaction disability: An application of status characteristic theory. *American Sociological Review*, 1972, *37*, 648–55.

Cohen, E. G., & Sharan, S. Modifying status relations in Israeli youth. *Journal of Cross-Cultural Psychology*, 1980, *11*, 364–84.

*Comprehensive Test of Basic Skills*. Monterey, Calif.: McGraw-Hill, 1981.

Cook, T. *Producing equal status interaction between Indian and white boys in British Columbia*. Unpublished doctoral dissertation, Stanford University, 1974.

De Avila, E. *Multicultural improvement of cognitive abilities: Final report to State of California, Department of Education*. Stanford, Calif.: Stanford University, School of Education, 1981.

De Avila, E. A., & Duncan, S. E. *Language Assessment Scales, Level I*. (2nd ed.) Corte Madera, Calif.: Linguametrics Group, 1977.

De Avila, E. A., & Duncan, S. E. *Finding Out/Descubrimiento*. Corte Madera, Calif.: Linguametrics Group, 1980.

Deutsch, M. The effects of cooperation and competition upon group process. In D. Cartwright & A. Zander (Eds.), *Group dynamics*. New York: Harper & Row, 1968.

Durling, R., & Shick, C. Concept attainment by pairs and individuals as a function of vocalization. *Journal of Educational Psychology*, 1976, *68*, 83–91.

Egan, K., & Marsing, D. *Teaching the whip kick using a multiability group*. Unpublished manuscript, Stanford University, 1984.

Epstein, C. *Affective subjects in the classroom: Exploring race, sex and drugs*. Scranton, Pa.: Intext Educational Publications, 1972.

Fishman, J. A. *A sociology of bilingual education: Final report to Division of Foreign Studies, DHEW, Office of Education* (OECO-75-0588). September 1974.

Gamero, D. *Evaluation of a small group curriculum.* Unpublished doctoral dissertation, Stanford University, 1981.

Gardner, G. *Frames of mind: The theory of multiple intelligences.* New York: Basic Books, 1983.

Glaser, R. The process of intelligence and education. In L. Resnick (Ed.), *The nature of intelligence.* Hillsdale, N.Y.: L. E. Associates, 1976.

Goodlad, J. I. *A place called school: Prospects for the future.* New York: McGraw-Hill, 1984.

Gould, S. J. *The mismeasure of man.* New York: Norton, 1981.

Graves, T., & Graves, N. Broken Circles (game). Santa Cruz, Calif., 1985. Laminated sets of Broken Circles (at approximately $1.50/set of 10 circles) may be purchased by writing to Ted and Nancy Graves at 136 Liberty St., Santa Cruz, CA 95060. Each set is enough for one group of either Simple or Advanced Broken Circles; an average class will need 6–8 sets.

Hall, J. Decisions, decisions, decisions. *Psychology Today,* 1971, *5,* 51.

Hallinan, M. Summary and implications. In P. Peterson, L. C. Wilkinson, & M. Hallinan (Eds.), *The social context of instruction: Group organization and group processes.* New York: Academic Press, 1984.

Hatch, E. M. An historical overview of second language acquisition research. Paper presented at the First Annual Second Language Research Forum, University of California at Los Angeles, 1977.

Hertz-Lazarowitz, R., Sharan, S., & Steinberg, R. Classroom learning style and cooperative behavior of elementary school children. *Journal of Educational Psychology,* 1980, *72,* 97–104.

Hess, R. D., & Takanishi, R. *The relationship of teacher behavior and school characteristics to student engagement.* (Tech. Rep. #42). Stanford, Calif.: Stanford University, Center for Research and Development in Teaching, November 1974 (ED 098225).

Hoffman, D., & Cohen, E. G. An exploratory study to determine the effects of generalized performance expectations upon activity and influence of students engaged in a group simulation game. Paper presented at American Educational Research Association, Chicago, 1972.

Hunter, E. *Encounter in the classroom: New ways of teaching.* New York: Holt, Rinehart & Winston, 1972.

Inhelder, B., Sinclair, H., & Bovet, M. *Learning and development of cognition.* Cambridge, Mass.: Harvard University Press, 1974.

Intili, J. K. *Structural conditions in the school that facilitate reflective decision-making.* Unpublished doctoral dissertation, Stanford University, 1977.

Johnson, D. W., & Johnson, R. T. Conflict in the classroom: Controversy and learning. *Review of Educational Research,* 1979, *49,* 51–70.

Kinney, K., & Leonard, M. *Groupwork lessons: Geometry.* Unpublished manuscript, Stanford University, 1984.

Kirst, M. W. *Who controls our schools?* New York: W. H. Freeman, 1984.

Krashen, S. Bilingual education and second language acquisition theory. In M. Ortiz, D. Parker, & S. F. Tempes (Eds.), *Schooling and language minority students: A theoretical framework*. Sacramento, Calif.: Office of Bilingual Bicultural Education, Department of Education, 1981, 125–34.

Krashen, S. *Principles and practice in second language acquisition*. Oxford, England: Pergamon Press, 1982.

Lockheed, M. S., Harris, A. M., & Nemceff, W. P. Sex and social influence: Does sex function as a status characteristic in mixed-sex groups? *Journal of Educational Psychology*, 1983, *75*, 877–88.

Macias-Sanchez, M. *Instructional organization and academic self-concept*. Unpublished doctoral dissertation, Stanford University, 1982.

Marquis, A., & Cooper, C. Peer interaction and learning in cooperative settings. Paper presented at the Second International Conference on Cooperation in Education, Provo, Utah, July 1982.

Morris, R. *A normative intervention to equalize participation in task-oriented groups*. Unpublished doctoral dissertation, Stanford University, 1977.

Murray, F. Acquisition of conservation through social interaction. *Developmental Psychology*, 1972, *6*, 1–6.

National Commission on Excellence in Education. *A nation at risk*. Washington, D.C.: U.S. Government Printing Office, 1983.

National Council of Teachers of Mathematics. *An agenda for action: Recommendations for school mathematics of the 1980's*. Reston, Va.: Author, 1980.

Navarrete, C. *Finding Out/Descubrimiento: A developmental approach to language and culture in a bilingual elementary classroom*. Unpublished manuscript, 1980.

Navarrete, C. *Problem resolution in small group interaction: A bilingual classroom study*. Unpublished doctoral dissertation, Stanford University, 1985.

Navarrete, C., Cohen, E. G., De Avila, E., Benton, J., Lotan, R., & Parchment, C. *Finding Out/Descubrimiento: Implementation Manual*. Stanford, Calif.: Stanford University, Program for Complex Instruction, 1985.

Neves, A. *The effect of various input on the second language acquisition of Mexican American children in nine elementary school classrooms*. Unpublished doctoral dissertation, Stanford University, 1983.

Oren, D. *Classroom structure and attributions: The effects of structural characteristics on attributional tendencies*. Unpublished doctoral dissertation, Stanford University, 1980.

Payne, D., & Strutner, P. *Money supply and inflation: An exercise in multi-ability groups*. Unpublished manuscript, Stanford University, 1984.

Perrow, C. B. A framework for the comparative analysis of organizations. *American Sociological Review*, 1961, *32*, 194–208.

Piaget, J. *Play, dreams and imitation in childhood*. New York: Norton, 1951.

Piaget, J. *Science of education and the psychology of the child*. New York: Orion Press, 1970.

Pfeiffer, J., & Jones, J. E. *A handbook of structural experiences for human relations training*. Vol. 1. Iowa City, Iowa: University Associated Press, 1970.

Resnick, L. B. Introduction: Changing conceptions of intelligence. In L. B. Resnick (Ed.), *The nature of intelligence*. Hillsdale, N.Y.: L. E. Associates, 1976.

Robbins, A. *Fostering equal-status interaction through the establishment of consistent staff behaviors and appropriate situational norms*. Unpublished doctoral dissertation, Stanford University, 1977.

Rosenholtz, S. J. *The multiple ability curriculum: An intervention against the self-fulfilling prophecy*. Unpublished doctoral dissertation, Stanford University, 1977.

Rosenholtz, S. J. Treating problems of academic status. In J. Berger & M. Zelditch, Jr. (Eds.), *Status, rewards, and influence*. San Francisco, Calif.: Jossey Bass, 1985.

Rosenholtz, S. J., & Cohen, E. G. Status in the eye of the beholder. In J. Berger & M. Zelditch, Jr. (Eds.), *Status, rewards, and influence*. San Francisco, Calif.: Jossey Bass, 1985.

Rosenholtz, S. J., & Rosenholtz, S. H. Classroom organization and the perception of ability. *Sociology of Education*, 1981, *54*, 132–40.

Rosenholtz, S. J., & Wilson, B. The effects of classroom structure on shared perceptions of ability. *American Educational Research Journal*, 1980, *17*, 175–82.

Schmuck, R., & Schmuck, P. *Group Processes in the Classroom*. (2nd ed.) Dubuque, Iowa: William C. Brown, 1979.

Sharan, S., & Hertz-Lazarowitz, R. A group investigation method of cooperative learning in the classroom. In S. Sharan, A. P. Hare, C. Webb, & R. Hertz-Lazarowitz (Eds.), *Contributions to the study of cooperation in education*. Provo, Utah: Brigham Young University Press, 1980.

Sharan, S., Hertz-Lazarowitz, R., & Ackerman, Z. Academic achievement of elementary school children in small group versus whole-class instruction. *Journal of Experimental Education*, 1980, *48*, 125–29.

Sharan, S., & Sharan, Y. *Small-Group Teaching*. Englewood Cliffs, N.J.: Educational Technology Publications, 1976.

Simon, S., Howe, L. W., & Kirshenbaum, H. *Values clarification*. New York: Hart Publishing, 1972.

Slavin, R. E. *Cooperative learning*. New York: Longmann, 1983.

Snow, R. E. Theory and method of research on aptitude processes. *Intelligence*, 1978, *2*, 225–78.

Stevenson, B. *An analysis of the relationship of student-student consultation to academic performance in differentiated classroom settings*. Unpublished doctoral dissertation, Stanford University, 1982.

Tammivaara, J. The effects of task structure on beliefs about competence and participation in small groups. *Sociology of Education*, 1982, *55*, 212–22.

Tyler, L. The intelligence we test—An evolving concept. In L. Resnick (Ed.), *The nature of intelligence*. Hillsdale, N.Y.: L. E. Associates, 1976.

Walton, S. To democratize science: Curricula for "Citizens" would emphasize applications. *Education Week*, 1983, July 27, 16–17.

Webb, N. M. Interaction and learning in small groups. *Review of Educational Research*, 1982, *52*, 421–45.

Wilcox, M. *Comparison of elementary school children's interaction in teacher-led and student-led small groups*. Unpublished doctoral dissertation, Stanford University, 1972.

# Index

185